Muslims in Singapore

This book examines Muslims in Singapore, analysing their habits, practices and dispositions towards everyday life, and also their role within the broader framework of the secularist Singapore state and the cultural dominance of its Chinese elite, who are predominantly Buddhist and Christian. Singapore has a highly unusual approach to issues of religious diversity and multiculturalism, adopting a policy of deliberately 'managing religions' – including Islam – in an attempt to achieve orderly and harmonious relations between different racial and religious groups. This has encompassed implicit and explicit policies of containment and 'enclavement' of Muslims, and also the more positive policy of 'upgrading' Muslims through paternalist strategies of education, training and improvement, including the modernization of *madrasah* education in both content and orientation. This book examines how this system has operated in practice, and evaluates its successes and failures. In particular, it explores the attitudes and reactions of Muslims themselves across all spheres of everyday life, including dining and maintaining halal-vigilance; education and dress code; and practices of courtship, sex and marriage. It also considers the impact of wider international developments, including 9/11, fear of terrorism and the associated stigmatization of Muslims; and developments within Southeast Asia such as the *Jemaah Islamiyah* terrorist attacks and the Islamization of Malaysia and Indonesia. This study has more general implications for political strategies and public policies in multicultural societies that are deeply divided along ethno-religious lines.

Kamaludeen Mohamed Nasir is a PhD candidate at the University of Western Sydney, Australia, and is co-author of *Muslims as Minorities: History and Social Realities of Muslims in Singapore*.

Alexius A. Pereira is Assistant Professor of the Department of Sociology, National University of Singapore, and is the author of *State Collaboration and Development Strategies in China* (also published by Routledge).

Bryan S. Turner was Professor of Sociology in the Asia Research Institute of the National University of Singapore (2005–09), and is currently the Alona Evans Distinguished Visiting Professor of Sociology at Wellesley College, USA, and Director of the Centre for the Study of Contemporary Muslim Societies at the University of Western Sydney, Australia. He most recently co-edited *Religious Diversity and Civil Society*.

Routledge Contemporary Southeast Asia Series

1 **Land Tenure, Conservation and Development in Southeast Asia**
Peter Eaton

2 **The Politics of Indonesia-Malaysia Relations**
One kin, two nations
Joseph Chinyong Liow

3 **Governance and Civil Society in Myanmar**
Education, health and environment
Helen James

4 **Regionalism in Post-Suharto Indonesia**
Edited by Maribeth Erb, Priyambudi Sulistiyanto and Carole Faucher

5 **Living with Transition in Laos**
Market integration in Southeast Asia
Jonathan Rigg

6 **Christianity, Islam and Nationalism in Indonesia**
Charles E. Farhadian

7 **Violent Conflicts in Indonesia**
Analysis, representation, resolution
Edited by Charles A. Coppel

8 **Revolution, Reform and Regionalism in Southeast Asia**
Cambodia, Laos and Vietnam
Ronald Bruce St John

9 **The Politics of Tyranny in Singapore and Burma**
Aristotle and the rhetoric of benevolent despotism
Stephen McCarthy

Muslims in Singapore

Piety, politics and policies

**Kamaludeen Mohamed Nasir,
Alexius A. Pereira and
Bryan S. Turner**

 Routledge
Taylor & Francis Group

LONDON AND NEW YORK

First published 2010
by Routledge
2 Park Square, Milton Park, Abingdon, Oxon OX14 4RN

Simultaneously published in the USA and Canada
by Routledge
270 Madison Avenue, New York, NY 10016

Routledge is an imprint of the Taylor & Francis Group, an informa business

© 2010 Kamaludeen Mohamed Nasir, Alexius A. Pereira and Bryan S. Turner

Typeset in Times New Roman by Swales and Willis Ltd, Exeter, Devon
Printed and bound in Great Britain by The MPG Group

British Library Cataloguing in Publication Data
A catalogue record for this book is available from the British Library

Library of Congress Cataloging in Publication Data
A catalog record for this book has been requested

ISBN 10: 0–415–47647–X (hbk)
ISBN 10: 0–203–87255–X (ebk)

ISBN 13: 978–0–415–47647–8 (hbk)
ISBN 13: 978–0–203–87255–0 (ebk)

Contents

Tables

Acknowledgements

We would like to thank Barbara Andaya, Clive Kessler and Tariq Modood for preparing the promotional statements for the jacket cover. We would also like to thank Loy Xingjian for taking the photograph used on the cover.

Part of the research for this book was supported by the National University of Singapore Academic Research Fund for the research project 'Social Distance in Plural Societies'. We would like to thank Fatma Binte Osman for conducting some of the interviews. We are grateful to Nguyen Kim Hoa who skilfully produced the index list.

Bryan S. Turner also wishes to thank the researchers in the Asia Research Institute at the National University of Singapore for helpful comments on papers he has presented at their workshops and seminars where these ideas were first delivered.

Chapter four (Social Distancing) is a substantially rewritten and revised version of an article that originally appeared in Kamaludeen Mohamed Nasir and Alexius A. Pereira, 'Defensive dining: notes on the public dining experiences in Singapore', *Contemporary Islam*, volume 2 (1) 2008, pp. 61–73, with the kind permission of Springer Science and Business Media.

1 Introduction
Muslims in multicultural Singapore

Introduction

There is much talk in the academic and popular press of 'the crisis of liberalism'. While liberalism is associated with tolerance, especially religious tolerance, religious conflict appears to permeate modern politics in both Europe and Asia. In particular, there is the widely held view that the traditional separation of the church and the state (or sacred and profane) is no longer relevant or even workable in modern multicultural and multifaith societies. Liberal tolerance in the West in the late seventeenth century was a response to the religious wars that had so profoundly disturbed the peace in Europe. The famous Treaty of Westphalia of 1648 brought to an end the Thirty Years' War and promised to bring to a conclusion the dynastic competition of Europe and the conflicts between Protestant and Catholic communities. The Treaty recognized the right of princes to determine which faith would predominate in their lands; it sought to make religion a matter of private conscience rather than public identity; it confirmed the dominance of Protestantism in northern Germany and Catholicism in southern Germany; and finally Calvinism was given the same status as Lutheranism. Princes had the right to expel religious groups who did not accept the terms of the Treaty. However, since Europe's population was in decline, princes were looking to keep their subjects rather than to expel them. There was therefore a strong economic motive for religious tolerance.

What has this Treaty to do with Asia and in particular with Singapore? The answer is that Asian societies also need to discover and implement policies that will avoid religious conflict and the liberal separation of religion and politics has been one such policy option in the past, especially during British colonialism in the Malayan archipelago. While it is often thought that missionary activity and imperialism went hand in hand, in fact the violence surrounding the Indian Mutiny of 1857 demonstrated the importance of not openly associating British trade and colonial rule with missionary activity. Asia has experienced during the twentieth century terrible periods of religious and ethnic conflict in India, Pakistan, Sri Lanka, Indonesia, Malaysia and southern Thailand. Tragically the partition of India resulted in devastating communal violence and the tensions between Muslims and Hindus continues to undermine efforts by the governments of India and Pakistan to achieve a stable political accord. One simple lesson from these complex conflicts is that it is difficult to separate ethnicity from religious adherence since religion often defines ethnicity and vice versa.

Why has religious conflict become a prominent feature of modernity? One answer is that the modern global economy needs labour market flexibility in order to import and export labour depending on the local needs of the economy. Global migration makes modern societies more complex in terms of religion and ethnicity. Where governments appear to be biased in favour of one section of the population (for example a majority ethnic group), diasporic communities will often organize their political struggles around a common cultural denominator such as religion. As religions themselves become more global – consider for example the spread of modern Buddhism to France or Hinduism to the United States or Islam to the United Kingdom – it is clear that religious identities tend to be transnational rather than local; thus global religious issues tend to fuel local expressions of resentment or anger. The global protests against the Danish Cartoons (2005) would be a very good illustration of these conflicts. This study of Singapore attempts to look at these global changes in the relationship between religions and states by concentrating on a single case study, as it is our view these global issues are magnified in the Singaporean case. Here is a society that is very determined to be a secular state, but one that is deeply diverse in religion and ethnicity, and in order to achieve that secular goal it must manage its religious hinterland. Although Singapore experienced ethnic tensions in the 1950s and 1960s, the island has been relatively free of bitter religious conflict. How has it managed this?

In this study we try to recognize two major paradoxes of the modern liberal state and we explore the various ways in which Singapore has attempted to resolve these conundrums. The first deals with the problem of national identity. Most modern states are culturally and religiously diverse. For most states, this is due to the migration of peoples, either historically or more recently. When the modern and open labour market society becomes more complex and diverse, it becomes more difficult to govern. Singapore is a case where migration in the nineteenth century created a multicultural society; however, today, it must deal with even more diversity. Like many other modern societies, Singapore has a declining fertility rate despite all government attempts to correct that trend. It therefore must constantly seek to import labour, especially talented labour. With its current population at just over four million and with little opportunity to recover more land, the state has nevertheless decided to increase its population to just over six million. While economic openness results in greater ethnic diversity unless there are very direct controls on the ethnic composition of migrants, the state has to assert its sovereignty over society and it does this by creating the myth of a morally coherent and integrated society. Benedict Anderson (1983) has famously written about how nation states create 'imagined communities', and this creation essentially involves a nationalist ideology. Singapore like other states must find ways of projecting a common purpose around the state and a unified national community. In particular, it must foster a vivid and meaningful sense of what it is to be a 'Singaporean' rather than for example a Chinese person living on the island of Singapore. It must achieve a delicate balancing act between nationalism, internal harmony and openness to foreign talent by not creating the impression that it favours one community over another. The first paradox therefore is that economic forces create multinational societies, but political forces must create national communities. Sociologists occasionally refer to this nation-building activity of the state in terms of building the cultural fabric – the great arch – of the society as the real foundation of political power (Corrigan and Sayer, 1985).

The second paradox is that, while secular societies like Singapore strive to separate religion (as a private matter of the individual) from the public domain (of politics and economics), governments must attempt to manage religions. Due to the first paradox, they cannot ignore the fact that religious diversity without management will in all probability end in communal tensions, if not in open social conflict. Our study shows that, other things being equal, the practice of religious piety will create a certain social distance between social groups and eventually these social divisions can harden into separate enclaves. The role of the state is to manage such social processes in the interests of creating a social unity and where possible it should seek to convince its citizens that such social harmony is not simply artificial.

Singapore has in the past experienced racial and religious tensions. There were riots in 1951 over the religious identity of Maria Hertogh – a European girl who had been raised by a Malay family (see Aljunied, 2009). The government has since responded to religious diversity by preventing religious labels playing any overt public role. As we will see in subsequent chapters, the Maintenance of Religious Harmony Act of 1990 prevents the use of religion for political ends. The state has also been willing to respond forcefully to eliminate any seeds of religious opposition for example in its response to what it saw as a Marxist conspiracy among Catholic intellectuals in 1987. Twenty-two members of Catholic Church organizations who had promoted awareness of the plight of foreign workers were arrested on the grounds that they were plotting a Marxist revolt against the state. The Maintenance of Religious Harmony Act was designed to separate faith from social activism (Case, 2002: 91). However, the paradox is that, in order to keep religion and politics apart, the state must actively intervene in the 'religious market' to guarantee that religious services – preaching, teaching, healing, praying and so forth – are compatible with public security and nationalist goals.

In the Singapore case, we argue that this 'management of religion' has two dimensions, each of which is characterized by further ambiguities. The first dimension is the unintended consequence of creating religious enclaves. This is because the Singapore state categorically divides the population primarily into four distinct communities: Chinese, Malay, Indian and Other; this means that these ethnic identities do play an important role in public life. Furthermore, since these ethnic categories are also in practice religious categories, it means that religion is significant in defining public identities. To illustrate, Malays are typically Muslim, Indians are typically Hindus and the Chinese are typically Buddhist, although there are a sizable number of Chinese who are Christians. Thus, there is an official ethnic enclavement of groups despite the government's attempts to break these down by creating a national identity of being 'Singaporean'. The second dimension is the management of Islam in Singapore; this is seen as necessary, in part, because of the long-standing 'Malay problem' but also, in part, because the Singapore government prides itself on its technological rationality, ranging from urban planning to its family policies. Thus, the state feels it has a role to play in what we call 'upgrading' its own population. These upgrading strategies include everything from health (implementing mosquito control and encouraging weight control for obesity) to automobile restrictions to education (including policies on 'Religious Knowledge'). Singaporean authorities (and the Japanese, too, for that matter) have regarded individualism and 'shapeless multiculturalism' as aspects of western decadence, contrasted with the moral superiority of Confucian Asia (Harvey, 2006: 61). The upgrading therefore manifests itself in the state's self-assumed responsibility to intervene directly in the arena of religion, morals, reproduction and family life (ostensibly to make life better). In this book we focus on Singapore's strategies towards its Muslim population, as implemented through MUIS (*Majlis Ugama Islam Singapura* or the Islamic Religious Council of Singapore) and its related policies for improving Muslim education, modernizing the law (*Shari'a* in Arabic or *Syariah* in Malay) and its Courts, and seeking to regulate and improve Muslim family life. In this case, despite religion technically being situated in the private or personal sphere, it is heavily regulated by the state.

Although Singapore is a small island city-state in Southeast Asia where it is surrounded by societies that have much larger populations and resources, it is a society that is instructive from a sociological point of view. Singapore illustrates in stark and clear terms the paradoxes of liberal capitalism. While the dominant form of global capitalism has been neo-liberal, few Asian societies have fully embraced deregulation in economics and liberalism in social life. The idea of a harmonious society based on a strong state and Confucian values has been more attractive. Asian societies have by contrast sought to regulate family and religion in the interest of social stability. The Singaporean experience shows that any society that wants to separate religion and politics (in order to guarantee freedom of religious belief and practice) must interfere systematically in society to manage religions. The success or failure of these policies will have profound implications for the wealth and well-being of its citizens, and in the regions that surround the island.

Multiracial and multifaith Singapore

It is crucial at this juncture briefly to provide some basic information about multicultural Singapore. Singapore is a city-state consisting of a main island and 63 offshore islands with a total land area of 682.3 square kilometres. It is generally an urban space with a negligible rural sector of 9.8 square kilometres. A total population of around 4.5 million persons and a resident population of over 3.6 million were recorded in 2006 which makes Singapore the third most densely populated city in the world after Macau and Hong Kong. In many tourism marketing campaigns around the world, Singapore is described as a 'multiracial paradise', made up of mainly Chinese, Malays, Indians and peoples of other races (see Table 1.1).

The origins of Singapore's multiracialism can be traced to the economic policy of the British colonial administration. Upon deciding that the largely uninhabited

Table 1.1 Ethnicity in Singapore of Singapore citizens and permanent residents ('000) (2006)

Ethnic Group	Population ('000)	Per cent
Chinese	2,713.2	75.2
Malays	490.5	13.6
Indians	319.1	8.8
Others	85.5	2.4
Total	3,608.3	100.0

Source: Adapted from Department of Statistics (2007: 32)

island at the southern tip of the Malay peninsula would be a suitable base to establish a trading port in 1819, the British recruited Chinese coolies who had previously worked in Hong Kong. At the same time, the British also recruited many Indian construction and plantation workers from the southern states of India (Tamil Nadu and Kerala) to develop Singapore. Finally, the British also hired indigenous Malays from the Malay peninsula and the Indonesian archipelago to work in the civil service; for example, many Malays were recruited to the local police force (Lian, 1999). Soon after, Singapore became a thriving economy, which saw the arrival of additional economic migrants from China, India, Malaya and other parts of Asia, Europe and Arabia coming in search of their fortune. However, since the trading port was the heart of Singapore's economy, the Chinese eventually became the largest ethnic community on the island. In this fashion, colonial Singapore became a classic 'plural society', in J. S. Furnivall's sense, as it was a

> Medley of people, for they mix but do not combine. Each group holds by its own religion, culture and language, its own ideas and ways. As individuals they meet, but only in the marketplace. There is a plural society, with different sections of the community living side by side, but separately within the same political unit.
>
> (Furnivall, 1956: 304)

In terms of contemporary religious affiliation, as mentioned earlier, most Chinese in Singapore are Buddhists, Christians and Taoists, and most Indians are Hindus, with a smaller number being Christians. However, nearly all Malays are Muslims (see Chapter three). This is because Islam spread across Southeast Asia between the twelfth and sixteenth centuries, mainly from Arabia via the Indian subcontinent (Hodgson, 1974). During the thirteenth century, the Sultan of Kedah was one of the first Malay rulers to convert to Islam. Around 1400, the ruler of the Malacca Sultanate, Sultan Iskandar Shah, also converted to Islam. As the Malacca Sultanate ruled most of Malaya (and some parts of Indonesia), Islam was soon spread to most of the people in the region (Andaya and Andaya, 2001). This is why the terms Malay and Muslim are commonly used interchangeably in Singapore. Another term that is also commonly used to describe the community is 'Malay-Muslims'. Yet, there are also some Muslims in society who are Arabs and Indians (including Pakistanis and Bangladeshis), as well as a few Chinese or European converts into Islam. In total, Muslims make up around 15 per cent of Singapore's population (see Table 1.2).

Table 1.2 Religious affiliation in Singapore

Religion	Per cent
Buddhism	42.5
Islam	14.9
Christianity	14.6
Taoism	8.5
Hinduism	4.0
Other religions	0.6
No religion	14.8
Total	100

Source: Adapted from Singapore Department of Statistics (2001: 4)

While Singapore might be described as multiethnic and multireligious, the term most commonly used to describe society is 'multiracial'. This is because, since national independence in 1965, the state has in force an official policy, known as 'multiracialism', ostensibly to deal with this cultural pluralism:

Singapore is a multi-racial, multi-religious society. More importantly, it is a society which upholds multi-racialism as a fundamental principle. We set out to create a Singapore where each person is treated fairly and equally. Where nobody is either privileged or disadvantaged because of his skin colour. Where the minority communities have the space to maintain their own cultures and ways of life, and are neither pressured nor hemmed in by the majority community. Where the different communities live harmoniously together. And where all the communities benefit from the nation's progress.

(Singapore Prime Minister Lee Hsien Loong, quoted in
Singapore Straits Times, 31 January 2005)

Most observers agree that Singapore's policy of multiracialism was a pragmatic strategy that was influenced by local as well as regional ethnic politics (see Benjamin, 1976; Clammer, 1998 and Chua, 2003). After the Second World War and a brief but unsuccessful merger with Malaysia between 1963 and 1965, Singapore soon found itself a politically independent nation state (see Turnbull, 1989). Among post-colonial states, Singapore was somewhat unique as the indigenous people of the region, the Malays, found themselves as the numerical minority while the non-indigenous Chinese formed the largest racial community. It was at this stage that the newly independent Singapore government, which was formed by the People's Action Party (PAP) that had swept to power in local elections, implemented multiracialism, as outlined at the beginning of this chapter, as one of the nation's founding ideologies (see Mauzy and Milne, 2002). Even though Singapore's population is 75 per cent ethnically Chinese, the post-independence Singapore state could not implement a policy of assimilation for geo-political reasons. This is mainly because the island of Singapore is sandwiched between the much larger Malay nations of Malaysia and Indonesia, which might not take too kindly to the Singaporean Malay minority being expected to assimilate into

Chinese culture (Vasil, 2000). At the same time, the PAP which formed the government was staunchly against any form of socialism, which at the time was being promoted by the communist groups under the command of mainland China. Hence, Singapore's first Prime Minister, Lee Kuan Yew, opted to culturally distance Singapore from China (see Hill and Lian, 1995). As a result, the newly independent Singapore state opted for a system where people of different races would have cultural equality.

The Singapore state – as a highly rational and technocratic state apparatus – regularly maintains that multiracialism has been, and remains, necessary because of society's ethnic fault lines (Brown, 1994). It believes that the lack of social interaction between communities during the pre-colonial and colonial periods fostered a culture of distrust and competition, which was then exacerbated by the onset of decolonialization (Lai, 1995). This led to the 'many' incidences of inter-racial conflict, which occurred between 1955 and 1965 (see Ganesan, 2004). Thus, multiracialism as a policy is designed to address 'the problem' in the following ways.

First, it seeks to demonstrate overtly that no one racial community is especially privileged or disadvantaged. In other words, all groups have equal status as well as an equal stake in Singapore. This aspect was directly in contrast to Malaysia's *bumiputera* policy, where the indigenous Malays were constitutionally granted special and additional rights. In Singapore's case, the state wanted to show that no particular racial community was politically or economically privileged, not even the Chinese who made up more than 75 per cent of the population. Also, the Malay community enjoys no tangible additional privileges, even it was indigenous to the region. Many observers have argued that the Singapore government was simply being pragmatic in choosing policies that embraced equality between ethnic communities; overtly favouring either the Chinese or the Malay community would have led to even greater conflict between social groups (Vasil, 2000).

The state's fear of conflict between communities has seen the simultaneous introduction of the Presidential Council for Religious Harmony and the Maintenance of Religious Harmony Act in 1990. The Council comprises a chairman appointed by the President of Singapore, and not less than six and not more than fifteen council members (Maintenance of Religious Harmony Act, Chapter 167A). In the Council, two-thirds of the members will be representatives of the major religions in Singapore. The main function of the Council is to oversee the Maintenance of Religious Harmony Act. The main tenet of the Act is to allow the Minister of Home Affairs to issue a restraining order for individuals or groups who are found guilty of the following acts:

    a   causing feelings of enmity, hatred, ill-will or hostility between different religious groups;

    b   carrying out activities to promote a political cause, or a cause of any political party while, or under the guise of, propagating or practising any religious belief;

    c   carrying out subversive activities under the guise of propagating or practising any religious belief; or

d   exciting disaffection against the President or the Government while, or
under the guise of, propagating or practising any religious belief.

(Maintenance of Religious Harmony Act, article 8)

Second, the state introduced a policy of 'cultural preservation', where the traditional cultures of each community (that is ethnicities) would be encouraged and
supported by the state. Part of the reason was because the state strongly believed
that retaining traditional Asian cultural identities would act as a ballast against the
perceived threat of westernization (Vasil, 2000). However, the state was also eager
to demonstrate to each community that their traditional cultures were (equally)
valued. This reinforced the social status of each group. Towards this end, the state
has various policies to encourage the retention of each community's traditional
ethnic cultures, including the implementation of the 'mother tongue' policy in all
primary schools. Here, all students must learn their 'mother tongue', which is
Mandarin for the Chinese, and Malay and Tamil for the Malays and Indians
respectively, along with the first language of English for all students.

In a similar way, the state recognizes the importance of the major religions
through the designation of public holidays. For example, there are a total of 10
annual public holidays, where not only the major religions are represented but also
the distribution of these holidays is in accordance with the ethnic ratios of
Singapore (see Table 1.3).

Last, the state seeks to ensure that public life should be always racially (or ethnically) mixed. The logic behind this ideal is that a mixed society where there is interaction between various communities is conducive of social stability. For this, the
Singapore government has a housing policy which states that all public housing
estates must be populated according to society's racial mix, which means that the
maximum proportion of Chinese people that can apply to live in an estate is a maximum of 80 per cent, Malay 20 per cent and others 10 per cent. The proportions do
not add up to 100 per cent because the state does allow for some flexibility.
However, the logic of the quotas is firmly 'multiracial'. At the same time, the state

Table 1.3 Public holidays in Singapore (2009)

Public holiday	Actual date	Religion
New Year's Day	Thursday 1 January	
Chinese New Year	Monday 26 January	Taoism (celebrated mainly by the
	Tuesday 27 January	Chinese)
Good Friday	Friday 10 April	Christianity
Labour Day	Friday 1 May	
Vesak Day	Saturday 9 May	Buddhism (Chinese)
National Day	Sunday 9 August	
Hari Raya Puasa	Sunday 20 September	Islam
Deepavali	Sunday 15 November	Hinduism
Hari Raya Haji	Friday 27 November	Islam
Christmas Day	Friday 25 December	Christianity

Source: Adapted from Ministry of Manpower website (http://www.mom.gov.sg/publish/momportal/
en/general/2009_Public_Holidays.html)

ruled that Parliament must also ensure 'minority' representation; hence the introduction of the Group Representation Constituency system of elections (see Hill and Lian, 1995). Even in the sphere of social welfare provision, ethnicity matters. The underprivileged within the Chinese community can seek help from the Chinese Development Assistance Council (CDAC). Similarly, underprivileged Malays can go to Mendaki, a self-help welfare organization that assists the underprivileged in the Malay community, while underprivileged Indians can turn to the Singapore Indian Development Agency (SINDA). For public spaces, the state has always predesignated places of worship for the major religions in every public housing estate to ensure that there is equal representation.

Singapore's policy of multiracialism appears to allow each community fully to express itself ethnically and religiously. However, there are many contradictions that can be found in the policy of multiracialism. For instance, one inherent contradiction is that the state claims to recognize the culture of each community. Yet, the state has, for instance in the sphere of education, relegated the 'mother tongue' to being a secondary language, while raising the status of English as being the *lingua franca* for Singapore's diverse population which will forge a new Singaporean national identity. At the same time, another contradiction that arises from the vow to preserve cultures and identities is that if ethnic identities – such as being Chinese or Indian – are culturally promoted, then it would be difficult to forge a singular national 'Singaporean' identity, which is important for holding newly independent post-colonial states together. Furthermore, the Singapore state does not make it clear whether ethnic identity or national identity is more important; indeed, the state flip-flops between the two poles, depending on its own interests. An example of this would actually be the case of the Malay-Muslim community. Owing, in part, to the effectiveness of the state's policy of multiracialism and cultural preservation, the Malay community found a strong source of identity in Islam; as such, the Malay-Muslims of Singapore can be considered a model community that has successfully 'preserved' its culture. However, the state views that the community being too Malay or too Muslim would be 'problematic' for integration with the rest of Singaporean society. We will discuss this issue in greater detail in the chapters that follow.

Also, as the existence of the Maintenance of Religious Harmony Act indicates, the possibility of inter-religious conflict is ever present over matters to do with diet, dress, marriage and reproduction. Also, there are certain religious practices such as the veil which may be in direct conflict with official secularism of the state. For example, members of the Jehovah's Witness, who preach pacifism, might refuse to serve in the mandatory conscripted military service. By treating social groups in terms of their ethnic identities, the state indirectly categorizes people in terms of religion and hence we might argue that one consequence of the state's policies is to bring about an enclavement of society. While the Singapore state has policies to prevent the emergence of ghettoes (for example through its housing policies), the unintended consequence of its multiracialism is to create 'the enclave society' (Turner, 2007b), that is, a society which is separated and organized around an overriding principle of security. In other words, by recognizing – in a multicultural sense – religious or ethnic communities, the Singapore state seeks to discipline and control each group, so that they do not come into conflict with another. As such, we argue that Singapore's policy of multiracialism can be understood to be a variant of the British colonial policy of 'divide and rule', which also creates separate enclaves to maintain social stability within a plural society. Still, Singapore's social policies are generally speaking benign even if they are authoritarian. We can contrast Singapore's enclave society with an extreme form of malign social enclavement, namely, the Apartheid policies of South Africa, where separation and distinctiveness was for the purposes of domination and discrimination. We could also contrast Singapore with East Germany in which the Berlin Wall was a dramatic statement of enclavement (of two separate economic systems). In short, we believe that the Singaporean enclave society emerges from the technical rationality of the state which seeks to intervene in the religious, family and sexual lives of its citizens with the aim of creating an efficient, trouble-free society. In such a setting there is little direct challenge, such as cultural or religious claims, to the authority of the state.

The whole reason why we posit that the Singapore state chooses to manage religions so tightly is because it believes that religion can threaten social stability. However, it is equally clear that social stability is not an end in itself but only a means; the ultimate goal is capital accumulation or economic growth. Singapore is an island city-state with no natural economic resources. To ensure Singapore's economic survival, the state implemented an economic policy that centred around establishing the island as a regional manufacturing hub (Pereira, 2000). However, in order to encourage multinational corporations to set up operations in Singapore, in addition to the many fiscal incentives on offer to firms, the state had to ensure that production would not be interrupted. Towards this end, the state introduced a series of new laws that virtually eliminated labour stoppages – including allowing firms to fire and replace striking workers – it also promised the investors social stability. For Singapore, the few years leading up to independence not only saw race and religious conflict (as mentioned earlier), but the PAP-led government faced political challenges from the left (see Mauzy and Milne, 2002). To eliminate this threat, the PAP government collaborated with the British colonial government to jail all pro-socialist members of the opposition political party. Since 1965, the PAP has ruled Singapore uninterrupted. For almost 20 years after 1965, it was the only party in parliament; it was only after 1981 that one seat was lost to a member of an opposition party. It was under these conditions that Singapore has been described as being an 'illiberal democracy', where 'authoritarian capitalism' is practiced (Hill and Lian, 1995).

The outcome of the state's interventionist and pro-business position is rapid economic growth. Singapore's per capita gross domestic product (GDP) of S$1,306 (approximately US$427) and a 14 per cent unemployment rate in 1960, increased to a per capita GDP of about S$39,683 (approximately US$23,000) in 2000; by as early as 1970, Singapore's unemployment averaged at less than 4 per cent (Singapore Department of Statistics, 2007). In the words of Singapore's first Prime Minister, Lee Kuan Yew, Singapore had gone 'from Third World to First', which not coincidentally was the title of his autobiography (Lee 2001). A few 'downturn' years aside – notably in 1986, when there was the 'oil shock' and in 1997 during the 'Asian Financial Crisis' – Singapore's economic growth has remained around 10 per cent per annum. Not surprisingly, this has led many ordinary Singaporeans to internalize and expect the state to continue providing 'the good life'. However, for themselves, most have accepted a syndrome of bourgeois *kiasu*-ism – *kiasu* is a term from the Chinese dialect of Hokkien *(Fujian)* which means 'fearful of losing or falling behind' – that is 'an acceptance of ruthless personal advancement and rapacious acquisition so long as one outwardly remains anonymous and conform-ist' (Case, 2002: 89). Thus, the state's policies, regardless of whether they involve suppressing political dissent or the enclavement of society, are tolerated by nearly everyone because they solve the social problem of diversity in the interests of economic growth. In the sphere of religion, we therefore argue that the Singapore government's strategy to maintain its control and social stability is to 'divide and rule' or to 'enclave' religions.

While we posited that state activity at the macro level can create 'the enclave society', there are also interpersonal practices (in religion) that can re-enforce the social distance between people. We argue that piety, or deep personal religiosity, may thus contribute to divisions and tensions between social groups. The social dis-tance between social groups can be understood as emerging from two inter-related practices, namely, the 'rituals of intimacy', and the 'practice of piety'. These processes are discussed in greater detail in the following chapters. However to offer a brief statement of the theory of religious piety at this stage, we can simply observe that religions in Southeast Asia are now in a new competitive environment where evangelical forms of Christianity, Islam and, to some extent, Buddhism compete with each other. This competition is often referred to as 'fundamentalism' or as a process of 'fundamentalization'. However we prefer to designate this process as an intensification of personal religion or as 'pietization'. One manifestation of piety is the desire to marry persons of a similar religious disposition, but there are many other aspects. Perhaps central to the new piety is adherence to a strict diet. Now the consequence of piety is to sharpen the sense of separate religious identities and to reinforce social boundaries between believers and non-believers, or between insiders and outsiders. In the new competitive environment, there may be greater risk of contamination from the outside world – for example in the Muslim case from contact with pork or other unclean creatures such as dogs. Cutting oneself off from the unclean world results in social exclusion of various levels of intensity. Because individuals may find themselves in conflict situations between religions in every-day life, they also have to come to practice methods of coping with other groups and in this study we argue that these practical coping strategies can be understood as 'rituals of intimacy' (Turner, 2008). For example, concern over pollution, espe-cially through dining, requires various personal strategies to avoid contamination. Diet, veiling and marriage patterns are closely connected with religious observance and these forms of piety can sharply separate social groups in the everyday world. This book looks at dining, veiling, education and marriage; these are acts of piety that, while important to the practising, can cause friction between social groups. We explore various ways at both the macro and micro-level where the possibility of conflict is socially managed. One potential outcome of piety can be the growth of spiritual enclaves as a result of the social distance between religious communities.

Enclavement can be the unintended outcome of greater piety, but it is more commonly the result of the state practices. At the macro societal level, state enclavement refers to the separating of groups for the purposes of active and interventionist management by the state. At the macro level, enclavement more specifically refers to the state's management of religions and one strategy of management is the policy of multiculturalism. The paradox of modern secularism is that the state comes to promote religion as part of the rainbow of cultural richness that is part of a diverse society. Religion is promoted as contributing to civil society but this richness has to be managed, planned and orchestrated under the careful supervision of the state. This is an 'orchestrated spectacle' (Taylor, 2007: 258) in which the state employs such diversity to create a form of nationalism that can embrace such cultural diversity and richness, provided that each minority embraces the greater cohesion of the national state. Through these processes, multiculturalism is harnessed to promote the greater national unity.

Religious harmony or control?

We are not disputing the fact that Singapore's version of multiculturalism – officially known as multiracialism – is a key factor behind the country's relative lack of inter-ethnic or religious conflict; also, the recent experience of Singaporean society contrasts sharply with the situation in many other culturally plural societies where there are cases of racial violence. However, there are several further contradictions and inconsistencies in Singapore's multiculturalism with specific regards to religion; more specifically, we propose that Singapore's multiracialism has, on some occasions, instead of leading to integration led to the unintended outcome of social separation and enclavement. We intend to use the case of the minority Malay-Muslim community to highlight these contradictions. Although the everyday life of the ordinary Muslim in Singapore is generally secure and prosperous, we find that, owing to the highly technocratic and interventionist state policies, occasionally things become a good deal more complicated, especially for the deeply religious Muslim person who wants to practise his or her religion. If Singapore is a secular and multicultural society, then this might be a problem for the pious Muslim person. There might be occasions when the pious individual will encounter aspects of life that are contrary to the teachings of the religion in public, such as prohibited food and drinks. Thus, the central question of our enquiry is: do pious Muslims choose to exclude themselves from larger multicultural and secular society to remain religiously pure and uncontaminated?

In the chapters that follow, we will attempt to show how even the best laid plans with the best intentions can sometimes be waylaid or to quote the Scottish poet Robert Burns, 'the best laid schemes of mice and men, often go awry'. In the next chapter, we will begin with a detailed discussion of the main theoretical tools that will be used to analyse the case of the Malay-Muslim community. At the micro-individual level, we will examine the 'practice of piety' and the 'rituals of intimacy'. At the macro-societal level, we will explain the 'managing of religions' or 'enclavement' through policies such as multiculturalism, or Singapore's multiracialism.

In chapter three, we will give a more detailed history and profile of the Malay-Muslim community. Central to the chapter is the notion that the Singapore state treats the Malay-Muslim community as a 'social problem.' The chapter will begin by showing that the 'Malay-Muslim problem' as it is currently known was preceded by an earlier 'Malay problem', which essentially was an ethnic and class problem. We will then show how this ethnic problem evolved into a problem of religion with the increased piety among Malay-Muslims during the 1990s, leading to the community being accused of 'distancing' itself from the rest of society.

Chapters four to six will look at specific case studies of how acts or rituals of piety are performed within the Malay-Muslim community in Singapore. The aim is to show how sometimes there is conflict between the multiracial and secular sphere, and the practice of piety for Muslims. More importantly, we examined how pious Muslims deal with these conflicts. Chapter four is concerned with piety and dining. We propose that there is the concept of '*halal* consciousness', which refers to how Muslims adhere to religious food prohibitions. It argues that pious Muslims will have a practical problem in public life because, on the one hand, they believe in the importance of remaining *halal* (and therefore pure), and on the other hand, much of multicultural everyday public life in Singapore is not *halal*. Through an analysis of primary data gathered from a sample of Singaporean Muslims, we find that rather than performing social distancing, which might involve excluding oneself from a non-*halal* environment, our respondents have shown some creativity to engage in what we call 'defensive dining'. These involve practical measures to avoid contamination while also engaging in a multicultural environment. We propose that defensive dining is a means for Singaporean Muslims to remain true to their religion as well as participate in multicultural and secular public life at the same time.

Chapter five examines the views and attitudes of Muslims towards Islamic religious education. We try to explain the strong demand for places in the very few Islamic religious schools – known as *madrasahs* – in Singapore, leading to a situation where hundreds of students are turned away every year. We therefore asked whether the strong desire for an Islamic religious education is because of increased religiosity among Muslims. What we found, however, was that Singaporean Muslims preferred to enrol their children in *madrasahs*, not because parents wanted their children to be Islamic scholars, but instead because they found that the institution of the *madrasah* was much more conducive than national public schools for being a 'good Muslim'.

In chapter six, we analyse the special role of Muslim women in Singaporean society. Rather than simply revisiting the 'traditional versus modern' dichotomy, we sought to understand how modern Muslim women remained true to the teachings of Islam in contemporary Singapore. We analysed primary data from a sample of Muslim women that had high educational attainment in order to understand their views towards veiling, marriage and inter-religious marriage, and whether their piety resulted in social distancing between social groups. We found that there seemed not to be significant conflicts between being modern and highly educated on the one hand and deeply religious on the other. Apparently, Singaporean Muslim women were very contented with the 'choice' given to them to demonstrate their own religiosity.

The sociology of the body is an important theme in these chapters on diet, education, veiling and marriage. Maintaining the purity of the body and protecting it from pollution are important dimensions of the rituals of intimacy and acts of piety. Protecting the sanctity of the body is important for the discipline of the soul and hence many aspects of everyday life are potentially 'dangerous' from a religious point of view. Living in a secular society can create additional hazards for the pious. The religious have to distance themselves from such 'dangers' and strict observation of the *halal–haram* dichotomy is designed to protect the pious from impurities in everyday life. Avoiding pork, alcohol, and exposure of the human body become markers of piety in everyday practice. The veil in particular precisely because it is visible, separates the individual from others and thereby creates a certain social distance between the pious and those who are not observant. These acts of piety especially with regard to marriage partners and the raising of children can reinforce the separation between social groups. We argue therefore that social distancing at the micro-level can often interact with the state's implicit policy of social enclavement to create potentially divisive fractures in society. In the worst case such divisions can result in religious violence (between Hindus and Muslims in India). In other situations, these divisions produce tensions, stereotypes and uncertainties. Our book is about the interaction between state policies and interpersonal behaviour in a society that is based on the successful management of religions.

In the final chapter, we return therefore to the larger discussion of how avowedly multicultural states manage cultural and religious pluralism in society. By choosing an extreme form of interventionist multiculturalism (as seen in Singapore), we note that some degree of social stability has been achieved; on the surface, things will not immediately fall apart, as they have done in extreme cases in Bosnia, Rwanda, Sri Lanka or more recently Kenya. Singapore is a strong state which is clear about its objectives and one which is genuinely committed to the 'progress of the nation'. This is most evident when the state is confronted with aspects of its multiracialism policy that are in direct contradiction with each other. For example, Singapore allows Islamic education, but at the same time limits access to Islamic education. It therefore demonstrates that between 'cultural preservation' and 'social stability', the state opts for the latter. These contradictions are not unexpected. What will be critical will be how these contradictions are managed.

In this book, we will use, where appropriate, the Malay system of naming, both in describing individuals as well as in the referencing and citing works produced by Malay authors. In the Malay system, there is no 'family' name or 'surname.' Malays are named by their personal name followed by the name of their father. Therefore, for example, Kamaludeen, son of Mohamed Nasir, is named Kamaludeen Mohamed Nasir. In this situation, citations and references to Kamaludeen's academic works will be listed using his own personal name, in the text and in the bibliography.

2   Understanding social enclaves

Introduction

This chapter offers an exposition of the theoretical foundations upon which our analysis of the Muslim community in Singapore is based. We argued previously that a central concept for the understanding of the contemporary situation is 'enclavement'. As briefly described in the opening chapter, enclavement can take place at both the micro level, as practised by pious individuals, for example, in their everyday lives, as well as at the macro level, as a feature of the larger social structure and as a consequence of official policies. Enclaves thus exist at the everyday level, in state activities and as a feature of the collective Muslim community. However, we also stress that these levels, while different in their dynamics, are dialectically linked and mutually reinforcing. Part one of this chapter offers a discussion of micro-level enclavement, which we term 'social distancing'. We also propose that two inter-related practices constitute social distancing: the rituals of intimacy and the practice of piety. Part two examines macro-level enclavement, which we argue can be seen in the management of religion by the state. We also recognize that collectives or groups, such as ethnic or religious communities, may also practise social distancing, but social enclaves can also emerge as the unintended consequence of social arrangements. The chapter ends with a brief discussion of how these levels regularly influence each other.

Theoretical overview

In modern plural societies people are constantly confronted in public life by an array of strangers, many of whom will not share a common language, culture or religion. This plural situation presents individuals with social issues about how they should interact with such people in order to avoid offence or disrespect. How can we avoid the possibility of daily conflicts with outsiders, strangers, visitors or the social mass of anonymous citizens? These everyday interactional problems may be further complicated by religion, if interaction with strangers from different cultures raises the additional problem of ritual pollution. Although, as we will demonstrate, while sociology provides us with a wealth of research on interaction in the everyday world from Erving Goffman to Pierre Bourdieu, we contend that insufficient attention has been given to interactional problems with strangers where religious identities can be contested.

In this section, we argue that pious individuals learn various techniques as they go about their daily lives in public, or as Goffman (1959) would say, in the presentation of the self in the everyday world. As we have said, our focus is on pious individuals. Yet, how does one know that one is pious? The obvious answer is to compare oneself with other people. Piety in this sense becomes competitive, but also exclusive. It defines relationships between Muslims, but also with non-Muslims who are the *kafirun* – the infidels and unbelievers. If rituals of intimacy help to steer the believer safely through the maze of everyday contacts, acts of piety can divide the world sharply between insiders and outsiders – between the household of faith and the household of war. In principle, religious revivalism can therefore have very significant social outcomes such as increasing tension between social groups by sharply defining identities and distinguishing between pure and impure communities and spaces. The Singapore state is a secular state that divides the sacred and the profane, but it cannot ignore religious revivalism – whether from Christians or Muslims or Buddhists – where there are potentially significant social outcomes. As we shall argue in the second section of this chapter, religion therefore needs to be managed.

However, at this point, we are focusing on the piety of individuals. The construction of the pious self is directed towards strangers, but more importantly it can also be directed to other Muslims. The most obvious example would be wearing the veil – more accurately the *hijab* – which not only is a religious requirement but signifies that the wearer is pious. Veiling in Singapore is a very powerful religious symbol given the fact that many girls and women there are fashion conscious and some even dress scantily. Thus, the contrast between Muslim women who may be completely covered and other secular women could not be more visually dramatic. Thinking in Goffman's terms, these dress codes are not only aspects of competition (between the veiled women and the scantily dressed women) but they are also everyday aspects of a cultural spectacle (for the rest of society).

We are interested in how one remains a good Muslim in a modern plural environment that might be fraught with religious or ritual pollution? For example, when dining in public spaces such as a food court or restaurant, how does a pious Muslim deal with the presence of food items – such as pork or alcoholic drinks – which are strictly prohibited by Islam but acceptable to peoples of other faiths? We believe that the obvious answer is to engage in a range of practices – which we call rituals of intimacy – that can not only carry the meaning and significance of the religion but can 'cope' with the problematic external situation or environment. In this respect we follow the work of Bourdieu in attempting to understand the nature of religion as a set of practices rather than a set of beliefs that embody the dispositions of social actors within their everyday world or habitus, which we term 'the practice of piety'.

Singapore provides a rich social site for social research because it is a society in which there is plenty of heterogeneity but also a strong state presence that regulates much of everyday social reality. The Singapore state does not take multiculturalism for granted but seeks to manage and control the complexity through its migration and residence rules, its legislation against racial vilification, its urban housing policy and finally through the specific arrangements it has created to oversee the lives of Muslims. We call these arrangements a policy of 'managing religions' and we argue that one cannot understand the everyday lives of Muslims in Singapore without looking at the state and its institutions such as MUIS. Our study of Muslims in Singapore starts therefore with the everyday world, but it concludes with an examination of those institutional arrangements that organize and orchestrate this everyday world.

In this study of Muslims in Singapore, we draw four important ideas from contemporary sociology as the framework of our analysis: rituals of intimacy (the norms of conduct between strangers in public places); acts of piety (the practices that define piety in everyday settings such as diet); the management of religion (the state's strategies for disciplining, governing or organizing religion, especially Islam); and finally the various ways in which intentionally or unintentionally ethno-religious enclaves are created that both separate and manage social groups. These four dimensions of Singaporean religious life interact with each other in various complex ways, and there is often considerable overlap between them. For example, wearing a veil can be a ritual of intimacy in telling strangers that one is a member of a particular religion; at the same time it is an act of piety in telling people that you have accepted a lifestyle that requires religious modesty. Piety can create social distance between social groups and hence contribute to the formation of social enclaves. Wearing veils or crosses in public places presupposes a relatively tolerant attitude of the state towards public displays of membership and religiosity. In this sense, the more these four dimensions overlap and intersect, the more they form a religious system of beliefs, practices, cultures and institutions.

Part one: micro-level theories

Rituals of intimacy

In studying the interactions between individuals and groups, we can call the everyday activities that are necessary for sustaining group identities and maintaining the continuity of the group 'rituals of intimacy' (Turner, 2007a: 63). This phrase has been coined to express ideas about social contexts and the expressions of self in public from the work of Goffman, especially *The Presentation of Self in Everyday Life* (1959). Goffman's famous study of the self as a public performance was based on his doctoral dissertation which was a study of communication on a Shetland Island community. At that time Shetland was made up of small agricultural holdings or 'crofts' that provided support for each family. We can safely assume that this island was in the 1950s a primarily homogeneous community. Goffman was especially concerned with issues such as gossip in a closed community where neighbours were often regarded with some degree of suspicion. Had Goffman undertaken his early research in Singapore, we can assume that the assumptions would have been very different. We are making the obvious point that presenting the self and negotiating social roles in a plural, ethnically diverse society involves careful interactions with strangers where there is a high probability of failed inter-action, embarrassment and possible conflict. It is true that Goffman recognized the possibility of misrepresentation and allowed for the disruption of everyday per-formances (Goffman, 1959: 57), but the Shetland Island had no notion of the dan-ger of possible religious pollution from strangers. He also spoke about discrepant roles, but tensions between social actors of different religions where interaction might lead to symbolic pollution involves more than mere loss of face.

Goffman came close to the issue we are raising when in *Behavior in Public Places* (1963: 124) he analysed 'engagements among the unacquainted'. The issue here is that in such engagements there is an open space that permits strangers to meet. For example in American bars, it is possible for two strangers to meet amica-bly and exchange conversations within this specified region. We would suggest that casual meetings with strangers in streets, parks, sidewalks and dining halls is indeed an open space but the openness can be threatening if we cannot predict the behaviour of strangers with some degree of confidence. Such casual encounters may lead to pollution if for instance certain dietary regulations have not been prop-erly observed. The openness of such engagements needs to be closed or at least regulated by certain norms. Dining with strangers may bring pollution if they have been in contact with proscribed foods. We argue subsequently that the response to these uncertainties in restaurants and elsewhere results in defensive practices that we call 'defensive dining'.

Rituals of intimacy can be constructed out of secular as well as religious norms. For example, the norm that one should not stare directly into the eyes of a stranger or that one should allow adequate space on the pavement for strangers to walk by or that spitting in the street is not acceptable are primarily secular norms. Aggressive eye contact is normally avoided in such public encounters. These norms which are designed to manage behaviour when we meet people in public places have a com-mon form and are widespread in all cultures – although their actual content may vary considerably. In this particular study, we are less interested in the generic nature of such norms and more concerned to understand the religious dimension of rituals of intimacy especially in the conduct of interaction with people who are not co-religionists.

These everyday rituals are part of the drama of representing the self, especially the pious self in contexts that may be ambiguous, contradictory or dangerous. These rituals or codes of conduct provide a series of answers to questions about how to behave towards strangers who are not co-religionists and how to maintain religious purity in societies that are secular. Following Goffman (1969) once more, we suggest that these forms of interaction between the pious and the impious (traditional believers or secular persons) constitute what he calls 'strategic interaction'. These assumptions lay the foundations for a micro-sociology of pious interactions, where two or more 'parties must find themselves in a well-structured situation of mutual impingement where each party must make a move and where every possible move carries fateful implications for all of the parties' (Goffman, 1969: 100–1). The interactions are potentially 'fateful' or at least 'weighty' in the sense that they carry within them the threat of impurity because they are designated as *haram* rather than *halal*. These strategic concerns are especially prominent where interaction between men and women are involved. The rituals of intimacy relating to shaking hands, dining in public places, appropriate distance from others, or appropriate flirting or courting behaviour begins to overlap with what we call acts of piety.

The practice of piety

The work of Pierre Bourdieu with its battery of concepts – habitus, hexis, field and capital – is especially useful in any discussion of the competition between social groups over authentic practice, namely over piety or correct practice. Bourdieu's emphasis on practice is important because there is often a bias in the study of religion towards treating belief rather than practice as the benchmark of orthodoxy, especially in the case of Protestant Christianity. Often Islam has been contrasted with Christianity because it appeared to favour orthodox practice (such as diet and veiling) over orthodox belief. This may not have been the overt intention of William Cantwell Smith when he wrote that *sunni* means orthoprax rather than orthodox, going on to say that a

> Good Muslim is not one whose belief conforms to a given pattern, whose commitment may express in intellectual terms that are congruent with an accepted statement (as is the case generally in Protestant Christianity) but one whose commitment may be expressed in practical terms that conform to an accepted code.
>
> (1957: 28)

If ritual expresses belief and belief is expressed through activity, then embodiment is central to all religious systems. Practice crucially involves the regulation, representation and management of the human body (Turner, 1991). The body and ritual are especially important in our subsequent discussion of veiling, dining and marriage where bodily practices become important in the social differentiation between social groups.

'Piety' is from the Latin *pietas*, which means reverence and obedience to God. It is also associated with pity as in God showing pity to mankind. It refers, in short, to habitual acts of reverence and obedience, and hence it is the habits or habitus of the pious. In sociological terms, the concept of habitus in the sociology of Bourdieu means the everyday practices that embody a set of dispositions which in turn determine individual taste, in this case a taste for particular religious beliefs, practices and objects. His work on *Distinction* (Bourdieu, 1984) was in fact about 'the distinction of taste'. In Bourdieu's notion of social capital, taste is determined by social stratification, producing a hierarchy of preferences (for leisure, for aesthetic objects, consumer goods and lifestyle). Bourdieu's use of the concept of habitus is ultimately derived from Aristotle who was concerned with understanding how virtues can be produced in individuals as a result of education, including the training of the body. Hence in Greek culture, excellence in the gymnasium was seen to be a foundation for the character of the citizen. The Greek word for 'virtue' in the *Nichomachean Ethics* is *arête* or excellence in which moral virtue is in fact excellence of character. The habitus of the individual involves what Bourdieu following Aristotle calls a hexis in which bodily dispositions embody both values and virtues. This type of argument has been recently applied to Islam, for example, in Saba Mahmood's *Politics of Piety* (2005). Although this discussion might appear to be focused on western notions of piety and excellence, her discussion of Muslim piety shows clearly the interchange between classical Arabic philosophy and Greek culture in which Aristotle was shared mutually by Arab and Greek civilizations – as in the commentaries of Averroes on Aristotle (Mahmood, 2005).

There is in many Asian societies a close relationship between reverence towards God and to parents. While piety from the early seventeenth century has meant devoutness and religiousness, it also conveys the idea of respect for parents and elders. Although we have couched this debate within western terms, we could easily present a parallel set of arguments from the works of Confucius and Mencius. For example, the latter says in 7A21:

> That which a gentleman follows as his nature, that is to say benevolence, rightness, the rites and wisdom, is rooted in his heart, and manifests itself in his face, giving it a sleek appearance. It also shows in his back and extends to his limbs, rendering their message intelligible without words.

(Lau, 2004)

In short, Mencius belongs to a tradition in which the self is the outcome of a process of self-development and hence it is a tradition which recognized the mutability of character. Both speech and bodily decorum are indicative of an underlying character and hence a set of virtues. Within a cultivated and disciplined self, character is expressed unintentionally through a virtuous disposition. Virtue becomes habitual in the life of the well-trained and disciplined person; virtue becomes as it were second nature. Hence for Mencius a noble character is expressed through the clarity and brightness of their pupils; an obscure look in the pupil conveys the idea of obscurity of character and weakness of virtue (Heng, 2002). This ordering of the self is also a reflection of the ordering of society in which piety is expressed in terms of respect for the elderly and the ancestors.

The study of pious acts is an important aspect of the anthropology and sociology of religion, because the spread or revival of religion in any social group or society requires some degree of pietization, that is through the reform of daily practices that give otherwise secular activities (eating, sleeping, dressing and so forth) a religious significance. Body and embodiment play an important role in religious belief and ritual, and thus pietization is aimed at excellence or virtue in the practice of religion. Mothers in educating and disciplining their children are critically involved in the inter-generational reproduction of these religious dispositions. The study of female piety in modern reformist movements is a crucial stage in understanding the modernization of the everyday world by the intensification of religious practice. By this we mean that piety is not necessarily the enforcement of religious tradition, since recent sociological research suggests that the mothers and grandmothers of today's pious women in Malaysia were not veiled and that the increasing demand for *halal* food and services reflects a modern not traditional preference (Tong and Turner, 2008).

Apart from his occasional comments on Islam in the study of Algeria, Bourdieu did not undertake a sociological study of religion as such. However, his sociological perspective is widely viewed as a valuable approach to theory and research on the body (Fowler, 1997 and 2000; Shilling, 1993; Turner, 1992). His work gave full recognition to human agency through the notions of strategies and practices, but it also recognized the determining role of institutions and resources (or social capital) in shaping, constraining and producing human agency. Bourdieu's emphasis on practice and habitus also lends itself conveniently to an appreciation of religion as a social practice which is shaped by the larger social structure or what Bourdieu might call the field as a whole.

We can define habitus as the ensemble of attitudes, dispositions and expectations that individuals share as members of a particular social environment for which Bourdieu employs the term 'field'. In Bourdieu's terms, taste is not individual, random or unstable, but organized in terms of social positions, practices and institutions. The habitus is an 'acquired system of generative dispositions' (Bourdieu, 1977: 95) within which individuals think that their preferences are obvious, natural and taken-for-granted. For example, a preference for Bach over Beethoven is not, according to Bourdieu, just a whimsical or private preference, but the outcome of training, conditioning and social status. Similarly he would argue that becoming a Zen Buddhist rather than a Catholic is not simply a random or eccentric preference, but an aspect of our habitus and the field in which we are located. As a secular sociologist, it is obvious that Bourdieu treats the preference for Bach as not different in principle from the preference for Buddhism; both choices reflect the dispositions of the individual in a particular social milieu. Moreover, in their daily lives individuals are not typically reflexive about their dispositions, because

> [W]hen habitus encounters a social world of which it is the product, it is like a "fish in water": it does not feel the weight of the water and it takes the world about itself for granted … . It is because this world has produced me, because it has produced the categories of thought that I apply to it, that it appears to me as self-evident.
>
> (Bourdieu and Wacquant, 1992: 127–8)

While academics may wonder why one community prefers Buddhism to Christianity, most believers are too caught up in the daily business of prayer and meditation to be too reflexive about the question 'why am I doing this?' Indeed such questions might appear irrelevant or even distasteful in the everyday world of ritual practices. For Bourdieu, tastes and dispositions are clearly related to our embodiment, and things that we forcefully dislike cause us distaste or even disgust. The seventeenth-century notion of disgust as an offence to our sensibilities connects this feeling of repugnance with actual nausea.

Habitus and embodiment are obviously interconnected, because 'the way people treat their bodies reveals the deepest dispositions of the habitus' (Bourdieu, 1984: 190). Our bodies express the habitus of the field in which they are located, and in his famous study of French status systems in *Distinction*, social differences in preferences for sports, arts and food were related to different social classes, and these social classes express different 'preferences' for body weight, shape and disposition. Whereas weight lifting and the cultivation of powerful bodies are part of the working-class habitus, badminton, golf and tennis are more closely associated with the dispositions of the educated middle and upper classes. In *Distinction* there are important connections between social class, preferences for food and body shape, because

> [t]aste in food also depends on the idea each class has of the body and of the effects of food on the body, that is, on its strength, health and beauty; and on the categories it uses to evaluate these effects, some of which may be important for one class and ignored by another, and which the different classes may rank in different ways.
>
> (Bourdieu, 1984: 190)

Because different bodies (strong and squat, lithe and athletic, voluptuous and sexual, or ascetic and controlled) have different aesthetic values in their social fields, we can distinguish between the physical and symbolic capital of bodies. Bourdieu identified social capital (the social relations in which people invest), cultural capital (educational qualifications) and symbolic capital (honour and prestige), but the human body is also part of the capital to which human beings ascribe values. Our dispositions are bound up with our training for and acquisition of a habitus, and hence educational systems are very important at the macro level in constructing the field of taste. Because in Singapore religious education in the private sector plays a major role in the organization of the community, we can safely assume that separate religious education produces significantly different cultural tastes between different social groups.

Can we deploy his work with equal success to think of the religious body as one where pious practices or investments have produced graceful outcomes? The habitus of elite religiosity generates dispositions or tastes towards the body that establish norms of propriety, gracefulness and spirituality that can be thought to embody charisma that is as a manifestation of orthodoxy or authenticity within the field of competing definitions, legacies and causes. These graceful enactments are the work of lengthy training, education and practice, and hence can be contrasted with the practical religiosity of the populace who do not fully understand and therefore cannot artfully practice religious acts.

Our discussion of acts of piety is partly inspired by the legacy of Bourdieu and partly by the work of Luc Boltanski and Laurent Thevenot in *On Justification* (2006) in which they explored various discourses (or 'polities' as they call them) by which the worth of a person is measured. *On Justification* considers the many ways in which the worth of a person and hence the different values that might attach to different persons can be justified. The most obvious example is an economic model in which a person's worth is measured in monetary terms. Modern notions about economics and the value of money and the market owe a great deal to classical economics. In capitalism, a person's worth can be measured by their annual income or their property ownership. The relationship between market worth and moral standing played an important part in Adam Smith's views of economics, sentiments and values, and it was for this reason that 'political economy' was originally seen as a 'moral science'. But Boltanski and Thevenot also recognize an 'inspired polity' in which a person is measured by their religious value or by 'grace' to use the language of Christianity. In this study, we propose that we can in principle measure a person's inspirational worth in terms of 'acts of piety', where piety creates a hierarchy of values or grace. Modern religious revivalism in the Abrahamic religions (Judaism, Christianity and Islam) has spelled out a new piety for lay people to counteract the unorthodox ways of traditional life and the secular lifestyles of consumerism in global capitalism. Pietization involves the spread of a new discourse of moral accountability in which a person's standing in the inspirational city can in principle be open to measurement.

Acts of piety typically involve bodily practices related to diet, comportment, deportment, bodily discipline and clothing. It is through such practices that one's inspirational worth is expressed. According to Boltanski and Thevenot, in the tradition of Christian sainthood, the carnal bonds to society must be broken if higher truths are to be achieved, since 'inspired worth is in fact indissociable from the person; it is attached to his or her very body' (2006: 88). The human body or 'the flesh' as Christian moralists have designated our corporeal existence must be controlled because it is through the flesh that values arising from other 'cities' are most irrevocably established, inscribing themselves in a person's body, practices and habits. Thus, the worth of a person in the inspirational city should be measured by the value of their acts of piety that are expressions of a particular religious habitus. It goes without saying that in traditional Christianity worldly success in material terms was often thought to conflict with spiritual growth, and hence in modern capitalism there are interesting issues about how in a city-state like Singapore, with its secular commitment to wealth, religious piety can be expressed in the new middle classes who have so manifestly prospered in the economic boom of the late twentieth century.

Ironically, we can draw some interesting parallels between secular economic markets and the competitive environment of modern religious revivalism. For example, there is a tendency towards the inflation of religious acts as the pious demonstrate their superior worth within the religious field. This competitive struggle over the 'price of piety' provides an insight into for example the pietization of women in modern Malaysia and Singapore and furthermore helps us to understand why there is a mounting conflict between the secular and the inspirational spheres. In writing about women and piety in Southeast Asia, we have been particularly influenced by Mahmood's *Politics of Piety* (2005). In her criticisms of the conventional perspectives of western feminism on the veil in Islam, Mahmood has also employed the concepts of Bourdieu to explore the growth and implications of the Muslim habitus for pious women in modern Egypt. Her ethnographic study of Cairo provides an excellent framework for thinking in more global terms about Islamic renewal.

In Egypt, of course Muslims practise within a predominantly Islamic culture in which other groups such as the Copts are small (and declining) minorities. Obviously norms of renewal are invoked more sharply when Muslims find themselves in a minority within a larger or more diverse community and hence where the pressures for secularization and assimilation are all that much greater. These group norms are more likely to be invoked when a religious community is a minority or where the majority feels it is under threat by a minority which, for example, is economically dominant. In a different context, Philip Taylor (2007) has shown how the Muslims of the Mekong Delta in modern Vietnam have turned increasingly to the pious practice of Islam as a survival strategy in a context where they have been marginalized first by secular Communism and more recently by the resurgence of other religions in the so-called Renovation Period. As a minority in secular Singapore, similar social processes may be important for Muslims in emphasizing religious piety. These everyday norms of pious practice then become especially important for defining religious differences. Piety therefore functions in the context of tensions and competition between social groups as a method of defining membership of a community. Where Muslims are not an overwhelming majority, there are issues in everyday life as to how social groups should interact without compromising their piety. One of the prominent examples is diet because piety involves above all a set of bodily practices for defining social relations that involve some degree of intimacy.

Gender relations are also a critical aspect of acts of piety because the female body and female sexuality are potentially dangerous dimensions of the everyday world, at least from a religious perspective. Being pious involves practices that avoid sexual pollution in various forms. The moral regulation of female sexuality is thus an important dimension of religious activity as such (Turner, 1991). The pursuit of piety often starts with the cultivation of virtuous selves through everyday norms and is expressed in gender-specific practices. These religious norms and practices have helped define not only religious identities but one's place in society. Acts of piety are partly a creation of modern times, where religious identities are becoming more critical and problematic. Such rituals of pious membership are by definition also rituals of exclusion. If a ritual defines a person as my co-religionist or peer, it automatically defines some other person or group as not my peer or co-believer. We might regard this outcome as a sociological 'law' of all classificatory systems. Émile Durkheim (2001) in *The Elementary Forms of the Religious Life* defined religion as a system of belief and practice relevant to the classification of the world into the sacred and the profane. Acts of piety in clearly defining what is sacred also construct a world of insiders and outsiders. In what follows, we will investigate how acts of piety are defined and employed by these Muslims as an expression as well as a way of cultivating religion, personality and identity in comparison to the world of secular others.

Part two: macro-level theories

Religious diversity has, with the collapse of communism and the rise of fundamentalism, become a major political issue in democratic societies, because we do not, in general terms, possess effective social policies and institutions to manage the social tensions that flow from increasing cultural complexity, and the conventional liberal solutions, especially the legacy of the Treaty of Westphalia which is the foundation of modern liberal policies in the West, are in a state of crisis (Turner, 2006a). In this section we consider the increasingly difficult problems of multiculturalism and religious diversity in relation to the state and the law, especially after the international crisis created by the terrorist acts of 9/11, and the bombings in Bali and elsewhere. Although Singapore has not as yet been the target of a successful terrorist attack, there is considerable anxiety in the city-state that such an attack would have devastating social and economic consequences. It is also obvious that as a secular capitalist state Singapore must be a potential target of some significance. Economically advanced societies can no longer rely on the conventional division between politics and religion, and have entered into a new phase that will have to involve the direct management of religions. In the current context of global anxieties over security, liberal states have evolved from policies of benign neglect to active management of religious institutions. In practice, these new strategies are primarily concerned with 'managing Muslims' under the banner of social pluralism and multiculturalism. These developments can be understood in terms of Michel Foucault's concept of governmentality, since managing religions is a recent adjunct of the more general functions of the administrative state (Foucault, 2000). Managing religions is important, if the state is to re-assert its authority over civil society, especially over those religious institutions that seek to articulate an alternative vision of power and truth, and if it is to command the loyalty of its citizens over and above other claims of membership.

Managing religions

As the economy becomes increasingly global, especially in terms of the flow of finance and commodities, states and their bureaucracies have in many respects become more rigid in attempting to defend the principle of state sovereignty. There is as a result a profound contradiction between the economic requirements of flexibility and fluidity in capitalism and the state's objective of defending its territorial sovereignty. In particular with the growth of a global war on terror after 9/11, states rather than becoming more porous and open have defended their legal and political borders with increasing determination. Singapore is no exception in a society that has often seen itself surrounded by hostile forces. Indeed academics have drawn a telling comparison between Israel (a secular state with an overwhelming Jewish majority in a hostile terrain) and Singapore (as a secular state with an overwhelming Chinese majority in a terrain that can become easily destabilized).

Singapore's ethnic composition is unusual in the Southeast Asian region. Most Southeast Asian societies – outside of China (which for the sake of argument also includes Hong Kong and Taiwan) – have a Chinese minority population. This ethnic minority is also typically a core element in the business class in Thailand, Malaysia and Indonesia. In the Philippines, the Chinese also married into the *lati-fundist* upper class. Although there has often been ethnic conflict between the Chinese bourgeoisie and the urban poor, the Chinese have been too influential in the economy to be completely excluded from politics. When Singapore was expelled from Malaysia, a state of siege mentality was prevalent. This crisis mentality eventually gave way to a more stable garrison mentality in which Singapore was sitting in a sea of Malays (Case, 2002: 88). Thus, Singapore is unique as a society in which the Chinese are the majority group within the population. State policies in Singapore, such as its policies on the family and more recently, migration, not only reflect the majority view but are also designed to preserve that dominance.

From a historical perspective, it is useful to remind ourselves that the flow of people as economic migrants has become more rather than less restrictive. For example, John Torpey (1999) has argued that 'the invention of the passport' as a method of surveillance and regulation is a product of twentieth-century statehood. In a similar fashion Saskia Sassen (1999) in *Guests and Aliens* showed how the free-flow of seasonal workers in Europe that had been common before the rise of nationalism and nation states was inhibited by the transformation of such guests into political aliens. While there may be an increasing global flow of goods and people, there is emerging a parallel 'immobility regime' exercising surveillance and control over citizens and aliens (Rumsford, 2006; Shamir, 2005). If sociology is to be criticized, it is not because it has neglected economic globalization; it is because it has neglected the rise of global security systems whose overt aim is to protect residential populations against the perceived risk of mobile populations.

The modern state has a contradictory relationship with multiculturalism and migration, on the one hand, and with security and sovereignty, on the other. In a capitalist society, the state seeks to encourage labour migration, porous political boundaries and minimal constraints on labour fluidity and flexibility. The state is under political pressure from economic elites to reduce the resistance of labour to the logic of capital accumulation. One solution to the resistance of organized labour to structural change is to undermine trade unions, make strikes illegal and import foreign labour to reduce the unit costs of production. However, the state also has an interest in sustaining its own sovereignty, and hence wants to create and impose a cultural and moral unity on society. Its economic interests inevitably produce social and cultural diversity through labour migration, but its commitment to protecting its sovereign power requires it to sustain a moral unity, to contain cultural complexity, and to assimilate the migrant, at least culturally. The modern state is an administrative order that seeks to maximize the social potential of its population (and hence it has an interest in supporting migration), but it also has an interest in the enforcement of a particular type of governmentality.

This contradiction means that we can expect state policies towards citizenship and migration to vacillate between treating migration and multiculturalism as aspects of economic policy, and constructing multiculturalism within a framework of asserting national sovereignty. While some sociologists have noted that 'we are all multicultural now' (Glazer, 1997; Kymlicka, 1995), much of the recent evidence from western societies is that multiculturalism is in retreat, because these policies have failed to deliver an equal share in social resources. More importantly they appear often to have divided rather than unite societies (Barry, 2001; Joppke, 2004; Levy, 2000). Recent political crises in Britain, France, Germany, Denmark and Australia have only served to reinforce this critical standpoint. The history of Singapore is somewhat different. As an international port, it has always been a migrant society and its Chinese majority, although a political elite, are also a migrant community. Singapore has been largely successful in embracing multiculturalism – or multiracialism to use its own terms – without jeopardizing the social supremacy of the Chinese.

Theories of multiculturalism have attempted to make a distinction between the social and the cultural dimensions thereby identifying four possible types, namely, cosmopolitanism, fragmented pluralism, interactive pluralism and assimilation (Hartmann and Gerteis, 2005). This typology suggests that multiculturalism can involve a variety of combinations of association and cohesion, including a situation where social groups retain their internal solidarity, but the society as a whole is fragmented. In this typology, social groups in a multicultural society can be in conflictual and competitive relationships with each other. However, in our view assimilation should not be strictly speaking regarded as a type of multiculturalism, since it is based on the assumption that difference is harmful and should be abandoned in the process of assimilating foreigners into a host society. At the very most, assimilation should be regarded as a weak form of multiculturalism. By contrast, interactive multiculturalism praises difference, recognizes group rights, and accepts principles of recognition and reciprocity. Cosmopolitanism involves a normative vision of this cultural diversity in which individual civil liberties are preserved (Appiah, 2006).

Multiculturalism is often a consequence of diverse patterns of migration and mobility. However, the argument against the theory of unlimited global mobility has been most usefully captured by Ronen Shamir (2005) in his concept of a 'mobility regime', which describes the paradox that globalization also produces new systems of closure and enclavement. There is what he calls a 'paradigm of suspicion' in which various categories of persons are seen to be dangerous, and hence their movements need to be contained and curtailed. Hence there is a need to conceptualize globalization as including migration and mobility but also involving 'closure, entrapment and containment' (Shamir, 2005: 199). The result is an emerging risk-management state strategy that has a global provenance. If we regard the rights and ability to be mobile as a legal and political resource, it is clear that the risks of insecurity are unequally shared by the population and hence there is what Shamir calls a 'mobility gap' that is somewhat parallel to the 'information gap' and the 'digital divide'. The economic elite has the power to overcome conventional barriers such as visa restrictions, while the poor are immobilized by their lack of resources – including the resources necessary to bribe officials. Finally, Shamir detects an evolution of these systems from certain elementary forms (walls and fences) to more complex systems (involving for example the use of forensic medicine and bio-profiling). While Shamir's contribution to this debate is valuable, we have two minor comments on his approach. First, his idea of a 'mobility regime' should in fact be re-titled as the 'immobility regime' and second, the notion of biological closure can be usefully elaborated through a consideration of the work of Giorgio Agamben (1998) on sovereignty and bare life.

We propose developing and synthesizing these general notions into a theory of 'enclave society'. We can initially distinguish two forms of enclavement. The first is what we shall call 'spontaneous enclavement'. This refers to the cultural practices of social groups that tend to produce an unintended social closure as a result, for example, of relatively frequent intra-cultural marriage and relatively infrequent inter-ethnic marriage. Second, there is what we shall call 'institutional enclavement'. This refers to the involuntary social closure of a social group with the specific aim of social exclusion. Furthermore, such institutional enclavement can be either benign or malicious. Benign enclavement might include the use of quarantine to exclude individuals or social groups who are carriers of an infectious disease such as SARS. Such closures are likely to be short-term or temporary responses to environmental risks. Other forms of benevolent enclavement may be the creation of geriatric homes to protect the elderly from harassment or domestic violence. Malevolent enclavement would be, for example, the use of concentration camps to control, demoralize or destroy a social group. Various social critics have characterized Guantanamo Bay as both illegal and malicious (Butler, 2006).

Global migration in the twentieth century clearly played a major role in the emergence of enclave societies. As we have observed, there is a central paradox of labour migration. The labour markets of the advanced economies depend on high levels of migration, because they have ageing populations. In addition, their own labour force is not sufficiently mobile and is often reluctant to take on unskilled or low-paid work. Singapore is clearly dependent on high levels of inward migration to provide a dynamic labour force for its economic needs. Many of these migrants, domestic maids from the Philippines for example, are in the service sector and others, especially workers from Thailand are in the construction industry. Singapore's labour market is highly regulated by work permits that provide for short-term employment.

Religion becomes an issue in this context because religious identities tend to be transnational, and offer alternative matrices of self definition that are not state based. There is as a result a tension between the transnational identities of neo-fundamentalist or revivalist religions (Christian, Muslim, Jewish but also Hindu and Buddhist) and the state-based identities of national citizenship. But the state also has an overriding interest in its asserting its own sovereignty, and hence wants to impose a unity on society in the shape of a great moral arch (Corrigan and Sayer, 1985). Its economic interests have the unintended consequence of producing cultural diversity through labour migration, but its need for sovereignty requires a moral unity. Given the conflicts surrounding identity politics and concerns over public order, modern states are giving priority to security over welfare and to public order over civil liberties. In part this situation explains the new emphasis on civic integration over the celebration of multicultural difference. The modern state is increasingly committed to the notion that sovereignty resides in the capacity to make decisions in a situation of political emergency (Schmitt, 1996). Enclavement as a security policy is a primary expression of sovereignty in excluding aliens from without and undesirables within.

In traditional Singaporean society and during the period of British colonialism, there were enclaves that were intentionally created as well as some that spontaneously evolved around social groups according to ethnic, religious and language differences. For intentionally created enclaves, the British colonial administration had designated specific areas around town where each ethnic group would be housed. For example, it designated the area around the Singapore river for the Chinese (this area became known as Chinatown), while the area to the east of the city – in areas today known as Kampung Glam and Geylang – was designated for the Malay-Muslim community (Yeoh, 1996). Yet at the same time, by the 1930s there were around 40 or 50 *kampongs* (Malay for villages) in other parts of Singapore that housed Malay and Chinese communities, as well as several housing enclaves for other peoples such as Indians (in Serangoon Road), Eurasians (in Katong), and Jews (Bencoolen Street area near the Synagogue) (see Yeoh, 1996). These groups engaged in separate trades and had their own domestic architecture and cultures. These are examples of 'spontaneous enclavement'. Although Singapore is probably one of the most managed and planned societies in the modern capitalist system, the Singapore state has not overtly employed strategies of enclavement to manage populations and has in fact embraced public policies to break down or at least disguise ethnic and racial differences. However, it does experience the contradiction between the need for labour mobility and flexible employment and migration, on the one hand, and the need for security and sovereignty on the other. It has what we might call 'implicit enclavement' by offering only short-term or highly regulated work permits. Housing Development Board (HDB) flats (that is publicly owned apartments) are a valuable social provision but they also allow the government to exercise detailed surveillance over the population, and thereby they constitute a form of urban enclavement. We are however more concerned with understanding the specific instruments of religious regulation which arises at least in part as a consequence of the ethnic and religious diversity that is the unintended consequence of its dependence on migration to constantly replenish its labour force.

Typologies of state responses to religion can be misleading if they are not treated as modest methodological and heuristic devices. The following typology of state management attempts to categorize government policies as either inclusive or exclusive. Obviously any one government may have several policy strategies in place simultaneously, and these policies may not be necessarily compatible or coherent. Governments are likely to try several strategies over time depending on local circumstances and the changing nature of politics. The more extreme state policies of enclavement involve the creation of ghettoes or social quarantine such as Guantanamo Bay or the apartheid system in colonial South Africa. These extreme forms of separation and exclusion can range from repatriation and expulsion to extermination and ethnic cleansing.

The repatriation of peoples is associated with the growth of national citizenship, the involvement of civilians as victims of modern warfare and the development of human rights legislation. After the Second World War, there were over one million displaced persons in Europe and in 1950 the office of United Nations High Commissioner for Refugees (UNHCR) was established, a year before the 1951 Refugee Convention. The UNHCR has in the first 50 years of its existence provided assistance to around fifty million people who have been displaced, both internally and externally, as a result of warfare and civil conflict. Repatriation has also been proposed by right-wing politicians such as Enoch Powell, a British parliamentarian who encouraged Commonwealth citizens to return to India or Pakistan in speeches he gave in the late 1960s.

We do not treat genocide or expulsion here because we are only interested in the policies of democratic governments, and there are various arguments to suggest that extermination and forcible removal is an unlikely policy in a democracy. While some politicians may recommend repatriation as a policy, such methods are rare and repatriation would be a difficult policy for a liberal democracy to implement. In short, draconian policies of repatriation, expulsion and genocide are incompatible with human rights legislation and would be difficult to implement because their very enactment is likely to contradict the rules of procedural justice in a functioning democracy. The laws that were enacted in Germany to declare that Jews were not citizens were in some sense extraordinary laws (Agamben, 1998). For similar reasons, the use of 'extraordinary rendition' by the United States security agencies appears to contradict the principles of rule of law upon which democracies are based.

Inclusive policies, although in some respects benign, can nevertheless be criticized as patronizing. By an inclusive policy of 'adaptive upgrading', we are borrowing a term from Talcott Parsons's sociological theory of social systems to suggest that some governments may adopt strategies to improve the education and social status of migrants with the view that such policies may help to integrate and domesticate such minorities by retraining its leadership with the long-term objective of bringing them into the middle classes. Parsons defined 'adaptive upgrading' as 'the re-evaluation of the older, previously downgraded components to constitute assets from the point of view of the broader system' (1999: 76). The opposite strategy would be to downgrade or even to degrade a population by transforming it into a minority whose main function in society would be to provide menial services. Degrading prevents a group achieving even minimum standards of civility. All under-classes could be said to experience degrading and again taking a phrase from Max Weber such policies would transform a minority into what he called a 'pariah group' (1952: 3).

Returning to our discussion on types of multiculturism, integration and assimilation are well-known strategies which aim to bring a subordinate or minority group into the mainstream, but with the implication that over time they will lose their cultural distinctiveness. These strategies are in effect strategies of domestication. The opposite strategy is to force minorities into various types of enclaves, including the use of physical impediments such as walls to stop the flow of people. Cosmopolitanism is ambiguous. It has been criticized by some as an elite strategy that recognizes differences but from a position of privilege. We challenge this

Table 2.1 Typology of state management

Positive state policies	Negative state policies
Inclusive policies	Exclusive policies
Upgrading	Downgrading or degrading
Integration/Assimilation	Enclavement
Cosmopolitanism	Cultural indifference
Politics of recognition	Politics of misrecognition

criticism but suggest that cosmopolitanism needs to be taken to a higher stage of mutuality that we can call 'critical recognition ethics' (Turner, 2006b). Although recognition appears to be an essential step in the development of cosmopolitanism as a moral attitude and a culture necessary for complex multicultural societies, there are, by that very fact, ample opportunities for misrecognition and resentment (Table 2.1).

We propose that Singapore's policies towards religion, for example the policies of MUIS, involve strategies of upgrading to bring about the positive management of religion. This upgrading strategy of re-education and development is paternalistic and very compatible with the culture of technological rationalism. We examine various dimensions of this upgrading policy in subsequent chapters.

Community enclavement

This study of Singaporean society starts with our attempt to understand the everyday life of Muslims, but our analysis concludes with the state and civil society. We argue that understanding everyday life requires an understanding of the larger setting within which such daily life takes place. We believe that the key issue in this larger canvas is how to secure consensus in a plural society; or put in another way: how to get social agreements and tolerance in a society that is in ethnic terms highly pluralistic. The problem of securing a social consensus that tolerates ethnic and religious differences has become the dominant problem of liberal democracies. Expressing this issue through the work of an influential legal philosopher, John Rawls in *The Law of Peoples* argues that social stability must be based on a reasonable political conception of right and justice confirmed by 'an overlapping consensus of comprehensive doctrines' (2001: 172). In a more sociological language, such a consensus involves some degree of social equality on the one hand and a degree of overlapping social networks on the other. In short, overlapping social consensus presupposes overlapping social groups. The site where these overlapping groups come together is in fact civil society.

Three ways may be considered in which sociologists have thought about securing an overlapping consensus: theories of civil society, social citizenship and social capital. In general we conclude that the preconditions of social consensus in modern societies are poor given the tendency of such societies to fracture around ethnic and cultural enclaves, and that global migration makes governance problematic in a context of weak citizenship. Strangely, recent attempts to rethink civil society are often blind to the role of religion. Because religions offer transnational identities, it is difficult to incorporate religious identities into national secular patterns of citizenship. While sociology prompts us to come to pessimistic conclusions, there remains a pressing need to consider how civility – consider the connections between civility, civilizations, cities and citizenship – can be cultivated between religious groups that claim exclusionary truths.

We need to understand how forms of social and political participation are possible in modern societies, namely what are the opportunities for social action, religious involvement and political practice in contemporary civil societies? In more detail, modern sociologists have essentially thought about these opportunities with reference to social citizenship, social capital and civil society. The concept of civil society is best understood in terms of the legacy of Antonio Gramsci. For Gramsci, civil society is that space between the coercive state and the dull compulsion of the economy in which social and political action is possible. Without a vibrant civil society, either the state is merely a coercive instrument or the economy blindly rules the lives of people. Civil society is that domain in which moral leadership can be formed and in the specific context of Italy Gramsci argued that the communist party would have to challenge the hegemony which the Catholic Church exercised over the working class. Gramsci's world may appear remote from the situation of Southeast Asian societies. Nevertheless, we also need to ask what can offset the coercive nature of state politics and how can moral (including religious and aesthetic) leadership be exercised in our time? These questions in fact appear to be very relevant to the modern history of Singapore.

The concept of civil society has subsequently gone through many transformations. For Hannah Arendt (1976) the rise of mass society meant the destruction of the possibility of politics and she complained that sociology was itself a sort of manifestation of the erosion of responsibility for our actions. She had a famous argument with David Riesman about the nature of individualism and the other-directed personality, and the failure of sociology to understand the conditions that gave rise to totalitarianism. The debate about civil society has recently once more assumed a dominant position in modern social science because the global neoliberal revolution, in reducing government expenditure on public utilities, can be said to have contributed to the decline of public life, and the rise of (what Émile Durkheim called) egoistic individualism and consumerism.

The problem of defining such concepts as civil society and public sphere has bedevilled political philosophy for centuries. Despite the definitional problem, we need a vital concept of civil society as the 'civil sphere' that is a field of values and institutions in order to create a space for social criticism and democratic integration, and such a sphere depends for its very survival on social solidarity, including an emotional substratum such as sympathy for others. Since solidarity is *par excellence* the subject matter of sociology, the analysis of civil society is a core interest of the discipline. Indeed the importance and the social function of sociology as a critical discipline are hitched to the survival of the civil sphere (Rojek and Turner, 2000). The study of this arena of social activity has been the topic of a recent major work by Jeffrey Alexander in his *The Civil Sphere* (2006). For Alexander, the civil sphere is bounded by what he calls the 'non-civil' institutions of state, religion, family and community, which are seen to be particularistic and sectional rather than universalistic and societal. The hierarchies within these social spaces often conflict with the processes of building solidarity in the wider sphere of civil life. The solidarity of the public domain is fragile and because these solidarities within the civil sphere constantly fail, there is an important role for civil repair, namely, those social and political acts that function to rebuild confidence, solidarity and trust. For example, the demand for justice, especially in modern social movements from the black civil rights campaigns onwards, is an important component of civil repair. For Alexander, John Rawls's *Theory of Justice* (1971) is a turning point in the development of modern political philosophy. However, he justifiably criticizes Rawlsian theories of justice, because they have little underpinning from empirical sociological research. Rawl's idea of an 'overlapping consensus' of comprehensive doctrines is a significant underpinning of his liberal theory of the state, but he offers no evidence about and identifies no empirical processes that might produce such a consensus. Some obvious processes would be high rates of inter-marriage between minority and majority communities, or the absence of residential segregation based upon ethnicity, or shared access to public spaces and utilities such as parks or municipal swimming pools. In other words, an overlapping consensus would require intra-group solidarities resulting in social capital and trust.

There have been in contemporary sociology a number of major works on the civil sphere such as Jean Cohen and Andrew Arato's *Civil Society and Political Theory* (1992). However, for Alexander, this work is flawed by its dependence on Hegel and Habermas, failing thereby to give an adequate definition of the civil sphere as a distinctive sphere of activity. Alexander argues that in the reinvigoration of sociological theories of civil society cannot be simply a return to the classical political economy of Smith, Ferguson and Hegel. His principal theme is that we should conceive civil society as 'a solidary sphere, in which a certain kind of universalizing community comes to be culturally defined and to some degree institutionally enforced' (Alexander, 2006: 31). Capitalist forces are not the only or most damaging threat to this civil sphere which is all too frequently undermined by racial hatred, misogyny, patriarchy, or by the monopolistic power of political elites, experts and bureaucrats. In these situations, social movements demanding a restoration of justice or a defence of civility and solidarity against the dominant ideological themes of economic efficiency and hierarchy of expertise can result in civil repair.

While political science tends to define civil society in terms of its formal structures and institutions, for Alexander the civil sphere is also characterized by key sentiments (reasonableness, calmness and self control), by civil relations (open, trustworthy and deliberative) and by civil institutions that are rule regulated, lawful and inclusive. The civil sphere is a space in which civil associations such as the American Association of Retired Persons (AARP) or the National Association for the Advancement of Colored People (NAACP) play a role in producing solidarity and restoring trust.

Our main discovery in this empirical study of Singapore is that in everyday terms there is a strong willingness on the part of Muslims to cooperate with other ethnic or religious groups. In this sense, the government's policies of promoting a plural society have been successful. At present, there is little evidence of any overt civil strife between different ethnic communities. However, there is very little evidence of overlapping social groups, mainly because there is reluctance on the part of Muslims to marry out. The rituals of intimacy protect individuals and communities from interactional conflict but at the same time the increasing piety of Muslim communities reduces their contact with other groups, especially as a result of dating and marriage patterns. Hence civil society is relatively fragile because there is not much evidence of ecumenical cooperation between religions at the community level. Religious differences remain strong and in the absence of inter-faith marriages, we assume these communities will continue to function as religious enclaves. Furthermore, Singapore is a low-trust society in the sense that the state takes the view that society needs to be steered or managed by state agencies. Urban planning, migration controls, policing, regulation of leisure and oversight of religious groups signify the planning and management of the civil sphere, but these activities also imply that the state does not trust the self-steering mechanisms of civil society. Lee Kuan Yew – Singapore's first Prime Minister – epitomizes this position of guidance without trust in his title as Mentor Minister. In Gramsci's terms, the moral leadership of civil society is undertaken by the state which takes a close interest in education, reproduction, family and belief. Under these conditions, civil society does not exactly flourish. Social gatherings have to be permitted by the state and criticism of the state is carefully managed. There are no viable political parties apart from the PAP itself. Although there is little overt sign of ethnic unrest, we perceive Singaporean civil society to be weak in a context where the state manages religions, but there is little communal overlapping in civil society. We conclude that Singapore is a society in which politics has been used to suppress the political. Singapore has many policies but no politics. Society functions because of good management, but also because a flourishing economy has brought sufficient material benefits to the (mainly Chinese) middle class and to the migrant working classes to acquiesce to the obvious imbalance of power and the permanence of the PAP regime.

3 The Malay-Muslim community

A background

Introduction

As we indicated in the opening chapter, Malay-Muslims in Singapore, as a community, have been criticized for their failure to integrate; the state has been worried that Muslims, owing to their religiosity, have been 'distancing' themselves from the rest of society. What is interesting is that this situation is not new to the Muslim community; indeed, there has been a 'Malay problem' in Singapore for 30 years. Still, there is something different about the current situation, which we believe is due to the increased significance of religion, both from the perspective of the state as well as from Muslims themselves in the past decade. As such, what was once the 'Malay problem' has evolved into the 'Malay-Muslim problem', with some aspects remaining the same, and some new aspects being introduced. This chapter provides a brief background to the Malay community of Singapore and then proceeds to a discussion of the so-called 'Malay problem' of the past three decades. We will then consider the rise of piety among Muslims in Singapore in the context of an Islamic revival throughout the region and show how an ethnic problem eventually became a religious problem.

Malays in Singapore

The term 'Malay' refers to the people who are indigenous to the areas that include contemporary Malaysia, parts of Indonesia, and the southern Philippines. In this broad definition, it may be common sense to assume that the Malay people are a 'race'. However, owing to the unfolding of events in the archipelago, being Malay has become much more complex. First, with the arrival of Islam in Southeast Asia in the twelfth century, most Malays became Muslims. Later, with British colonization of the Malay Peninsula in the eighteenth century, the notion of Malay identity was again contested. Eventually, in resistance to British rule, the notion of a *bangsa* (nation in Malay) Malay emerged, based on three pillars of Malayness: *bahasa, raja dan agama* (translated: language, ruler and religion). In this case, the religion was Islam. Most recently, Malays living in post-independence Malaysia have had to deal with yet another renegotiation of Malay identity, one that was intrinsically linked to the country's political economy (Shamsul, 2001).

The history of the Malay community of Singapore, although indirectly affected by identity politics in Malaysia, was slightly different. Since 1819, the British colonial administration implemented a 'divide and rule' policy, which was based on the British notion of 'race' (Turnbull, 1989). The Malay community in colonial Singapore eventually filled occupations within the lower rungs of the British civil service, including in the local police force and the local military regiment. The community was housed, as part of the colonial government's master plan, in the south-eastern part of the island, in areas known today as Kampong Glam, Geylang and Eunos (Yeoh, 1996). Upon independence in 1965, the PAP-led government adopted and modified the British colonial government's 'divide and rule' policy, renaming it 'multiracialism'.

As we argued in chapter one, Singapore's multiracialism not only espouses 'equality' of the races, but also ensures 'cultural preservation'. For multiracialism to be implemented, the state first has to recognize each race in order for its distinctive culture to be preserved. Thus, the Singapore government recognizes the charter races, which are the Chinese, and the minority races, which refer to the Malays and Indians. Minority races are given the following special considerations under Article 152 of Singapore's constitution:

1   It shall be the responsibility of the Government constantly to care for the interests of the racial and religious minorities in Singapore.
2   The Government shall exercise its functions in such manner as to recognize the special position of the Malays, who are the indigenous people of Singapore, and accordingly it shall be the responsibility of the Government to protect, safeguard, support, foster and promote their political, educational, religious, economic, social and cultural interests and the Malay language.

(Constitution of the Republic of Singapore)

To safeguard, support, foster and promote Malay culture, the state has intervened to manage their religion, which is Islam. For example, there is a Minister in Charge of Muslim Affairs in Parliament. Also, since nearly all Malays are Muslims, they fall under the Administration of Muslim Law Act (AMLA), and the *Syariah* (Islamic law, also known as *Shari'a* in Arabic) Court. Although it might appear that the Malays are acknowledged as the indigenous people of Singapore who have special rights, in reality the only additional right that they have is, in theory, the state's guarantee that their culture will not be eroded. However, as part of its multiracial policy, the state also has a cultural preservation policy, not just for the Malays but for every ethnic or racial community. For example, the 'traditional' language of each community is officially supported by the state. The outcome of this is therefore that the state has to officially support the culture of the numerically dominant Chinese community, since under Singapore's multiracialism, all cultures are equal and need to be also preserved. Hence, what began as 'special rights' for the Malays turned out to be rights that are afforded to everyone else in Singapore.

In addition, despite their officially designated 'special position', Malays – who only constitute around 15 per cent of Singapore's overall resident population – are not particularly socially privileged. Instead, the social reality is quite the opposite. Between independence in 1965 and 1990, the state has generally believed that there was a 'Malay problem'. The symptom of the problem was that Malays just did not seem to 'integrate' with the rest of Singaporean society. More specifically, while the rest of Singapore had been enjoying high growth and development, the Malay community was set apart by their apparent economic backwardness as well as social pathology, especially with regard to juvenile delinquency and broken families (Li, 1989; Lily Zubaidah, 1998; Kamaludeen, 2007a). In 1980, the average monthly household income for Malays was S$770, whereas it was S$800 for Indians and S$920 for the Chinese (Mendaki, 2007: 11). Another indicator of economic status is occupational stratification. In this regard, there were fewer Malays holding professional, administrative or managerial positions in comparison with other ethnic groups in 1980 (Table 3.1).

This outcome was probably the result of the fact that the Malay workforce generally held lower educational qualifications than the Chinese or Indians (Table 3.2). In education, in 1980 it was found that only 85 per cent of Malay children aged between seven and sixteen years old were enrolled in school, compared to 88 per

Table 3.1 Occupational stratification in Singapore by ethnic group (per cent)

	Malays	Chinese	Indians
Administrative & Managerial	2.4	14.6	11.4
Professional	4.6	12.6	18.2
Technical & Related	14.2	20.1	17.1
Clerical	18.6	13.6	14.0
Sales & Services	20.3	13.8	14.7
Production & Related	26.1	16.7	13.7
Cleaners & Labourers	10.8	5.2	6.8
Others	3.0	3.4	4.0
Total	100	100	100

Source: Adapted from Mendaki (2007: 23)

Note
Totals do not add up to 100 per cent due to rounding off of figures.

Table 3.2 Singapore's workforce by educational qualification and ethnic group in 1980

	Malays	Chinese	Indians
University	0.3	23.6	28.5
Polytechnic	0.1	11.5	7.7
Upper Secondary	3.3	17.3	18.7
Secondary	15.7	21.7	23.2
Below Secondary	80.6	26	21.8
Total	100	100	100

Source: Adapted from Mendaki (2007: 22)

Note
Totals do not add up to 100 per cent due to rounding off of figures.

cent of Indian children and 91 per cent of Chinese children (Mendaki, 2007: 3). In 1980, only 16 percent of Malay students received a minimum of five 'O' level passes, compared to 34 per cent for Indians, and 44 per cent for Chinese (Mendaki, 2007: 4). In 1990, 36 per cent of Malay students qualified for tertiary education (university or polytechnic), compared to 39 per cent of Indians, and 65 per cent of Chinese (Mendaki, 2007: 5).

On the issue of juvenile delinquency, the state has been most concerned about drug and substance abuse within the Malay community. In 1990, it was reported that around 16 per cent of the Malay community were cited for drug abuse, compared to 1.3 per cent and 8.3 per cent for the Chinese and Indian communities respectively (Mendaki, 2007: 16). Similarly, the state has also been 'seriously concerned' about the (relatively) high divorce rates within the Malay community. For example, in 1980 the divorce rate for Malays was just under 7 per cent, compared to just over 3 per cent for the Chinese and 5.6 per cent for Indians (Mendaki, 2007: 14). Malays also had a higher proportion of children born to unmarried women than the Chinese – 0.59 per cent compared to 0.25 per cent – but lower than the Indians (0.88 per cent) (Mendaki, 2007: 14). Malay female teenagers giving birth was 1.34 per cent of women, compared to 0.52 for the Chinese and 1.05 for Indians (Mendaki, 2007: 15). The Malay community's relative lack of 'progress' during Singapore's first phase of industrialization and growth led Wan Hussin Zoohri, a former Malay community leader and also a member of the ruling political elite (1980–91) to write that the Malays were the most 'ill-equipped and depressed (minority) community in a modernizing Singapore' (Wan Hussin, 1990: 1). Interestingly, some observers believed that Singapore's first Prime Minister, Lee Kuan Yew, had strong opinions about the reasons for the backwardness of the Malay community. Michael Barr (2000) argued that Lee believed a combination of nature and nurture contributed to the Malay community's inability to keep up with the other races. Barr also found evidence that Lee generally agreed with the primary thesis of Mahathir Mohamad's book, *The Malay Dilemma,* published in 1970, which claimed that the Malays were 'backward' because of a combination of culture and 'genes'. According to Barr, Lee had said:

> From that book I realized that [Mahathir Mohamad] believed in it as a medical man – that these were problems of the development of the Malay race, anthropological problems, and these were strongly-held views. Indeed, I found myself in agreement with three-quarters of his analysis of the problem – that the Malays had always withdrawn from competition and never really entered into the mainstream of economic activity; that the Malays would always get their children or relatives married off regardless of whether it was good or bad.
>
> (Lee, in an interview with *New Straits Times* (Malaysia),
> 14 October 1989, quoted in Barr, 1999: 159)

In the *Malay Dilemma*, Mahathir – the Prime Minister of Malaysia from 1981 to 2003 – wrote that the non-confrontational nature of the Malays (in colonial

Malaya) had allowed them to be subjugated in their own land by the other races with the collusion of the British (Mahathir, 1970 quoted in Barr, 1999).

Social science analyses focused their energies on more logical reasons behind the apparent backwardness of the Malay community. Tania Li's (1989) anthropological monograph dispelled many of the 'popular' negative and static cultural stereotypes, propagated not only by Singapore [state] elites but also by some academicians. Li had argued that the Malay community was not 'culturally' inferior, but was trapped by typical 'class-based' problems which were common in any community making the transition from traditional to modern society. In other words, the Malays were economically backward because they were economically less prepared than the other communities to 'grab' the opportunities brought about by rapid industrialization.

Also adopting a political-economy perspective was Lily Zubaidah Rahim's (1998) study. She suggested that the Singapore government's policy of multiracialism – that the Malays should be left to their own ways – was the most significant reason for their general educational under-achievement (1998: 23). She continued by arguing that:

> The rhetoric that Singapore is a meritocratic society where equal opportunities are available to all has also served to add legitimacy to the cultural deficit thesis which infers that Malays have not been able to make it in a meritocratic society because they have not worked hard enough and thus have only themselves to blame.
>
> (Lily Zubaidah, 1998: 58)

To summarize, Lily Zubaidah Rahim's critical political-economy approach put the blame for the backwardness of the Malay community squarely on the shoulders of the state. While we suggest that the state might be guilty on some counts, we believe that the educational marginality of the Malays up to the 1980s also has its roots in the community's rejection of English-language education in the colonial era (Kamaludeen, 2007a). In short, the Malay community opted to retain the Malay language as the medium of instruction in its schools rather than immediately switching to English upon independence. Thus, when the Malay community had no choice but to embrace English later on after Singapore separated from the Malay federation, there was a generation that was already in existence that was educationally disadvantaged (Kamaludeen, 2007a).

It is not our intention to undertake a review of the many causes of the Malay community's economic backwardness. Instead, the main issue is that the Malay community was apart or different from the rest of Singaporean society. More specifically, the state believed that the community either could not or did not want to be like the rest of Singapore. Typically, the state was quick to intervene to 'address' the 'Malay problem' and its most significant move was the formation of Mendaki, or Yayasan Mendaki, which is Malay for 'The Council for the Education of Muslim Children'. Technically speaking, Mendaki ought to be considered part of civil society, since it was to be formed by the Malay community for the community in 1981. However, it is well known that the state, together with Malay Members of Parliament, 'encouraged' the formation of Mendaki, which was Singapore's first ethnic self-help organization. The thrust of Mendaki was to improve the educational performance of Malay students, who were as a whole under-performing when compared to the other races. Using donations from the community and financial support from the state, Mendaki launched a large-scale after-school tuition programme for Malay students in the subjects of English and Mathematics (Stimpfl, 2006). In a self-realizing logic of its own, the improvements made by the Malays after Mendaki reinforced the Singapore government's ideological beliefs about the 'cultural deficit' of the Malay community, which in turn gave the state even more justification for further intervention. Based on this logic, we argue that the state's perpetuation of 'deviant Malays', or the labelling of the Malay community as being 'problematic', served as a source of what sociologists have called 'moral panic' (Hill, 2002). This gave the state the moral authority to intervene and to seek 'to improve' the Malay community by whatever means deemed appropriate.

Since 1990 the Malay community has improved significantly in all of the categories that the state set targets in, such as in the economic and educational sphere. State agencies also have pointed out that the Malay community has improved in the areas of drug abuse and marital dissolution. However, instead of disappearance of 'the Malay problem', at the beginning of the new millennium, the Malay community was once again seen as a 'social problem'. We argue that this new problem, known as the 'Malay-Muslim problem', is in part a legacy of the earlier problems, but at the same time, is new because of the significant involvement of Islam.

Islam in Singapore

Although Islam had always been a central component of Malay identity, the religion by itself was previously not viewed by the state as contributing to the 'backwardness' of the Malay community. However, it is our contention that during the 1990s Islam was viewed by some within the Singapore state and some non-Muslims as being the root of the Malay community's inability or unwillingness to integrate, albeit in a slightly different manner. Before we discuss this new problem, let us briefly introduce the position of Islam as a religion within Singaporean society.

Singapore is constitutionally a secular state. This does not mean that the practice of religion is disallowed or that religious beliefs are discouraged. Singapore's secularism simply means that there is no official state religion, nor does it give any religion special privileges (Suzaina, 2004: 362). However, while the state does tacitly encourage religiosity, it views religion as being a moral ballast for Singaporeans. It has laws – such as the Religious Harmony Act – that protect against overzealousness of religious activity, since the state believes that inter-religious conflicts might occur (Sinha, 1999). Towards this end, as we have mentioned already, the Singapore state – in its typically interventionist style – actively manages religions. While religion should remain with the private sphere, it is nevertheless managed from the public sphere. This is most evident with regards to Islam. This management is done through the institutionalization of the AMLA and the formation of the MUIS. The following issues which are addressed in the AMLA:

- *Majlis Ugama* Islam MUIS
- The *Syariah* Court
- Muslim Financial Provisions
- Mosque and Religious Schools
- *Halal* and *Haj* matters
- Marriage and Divorce
- Property
- Conversions
- Religious Offences
- Miscellaneous

Source: Administration of Muslim Law Act (1999 revised)
(http://statutes.agc.gov.sg/non_version/cgi-bin/cgi_legdisp.pl?actno=1999-
REVED-3&date=20080915&method=whole&doctitle=)

As part of the AMLA, MUIS is to advise the President of Singapore on all matters relating to Islam, as well as advise the Government on the Muslim community's concerns. The Government, on their part, facilitates financial assistance in the building and maintenance of mosques. More recently, since 1996, the state has also appointed a Minister in Charge of Muslim Affairs. MUIS's functions, duties, responsibilities and powers are clearly defined in the AMLA as follows:

a   to advise the President of Singapore in matters relating to the Muslim religion in Singapore;
b   to administer matters relating to the Muslim religion and Muslims in Singapore including any matter relating to the *Haj* or *halal* certification;
c   to administer all Muslim endowments and funds vested in it under any written law or trust;
d   to administer the collection of *zakat* and *fitrah* and other charitable contributions for the support and promotion of the Muslim religion or for the benefit of Muslims in accordance with this Act;
e   to administer all mosques and Muslim religious schools in Singapore; and
f   to carry out such other functions and duties as are conferred upon the *Majlis* by or under this Act or any other written law.

Source: Administration of Muslim Law Act (1999 revised) (part 2: 2)
(http://statutes.agc.gov.sg/non_version/cgi-bin/cgi_legdisp.pl?actno=
1999-REVED-3&date=20080915&method=whole&doctitle=)

Although officially registered as a corporate entity in Singapore, MUIS is a state-linked statutory board in all but name. It is powerful because it is tasked with 'managing' Islam in Singapore. Under the AMLA, the President of Singapore may, after consultation with MUIS, appoint the *Mufti* of Singapore. While there are many meanings of the word, the *Mufti* is essentially the most senior Islamic authority in Singapore. He is appointed on the basis of his religious scholarship. The *Mufti* sits on the Council of MUIS, along with the President of MUIS, and other persons recommended by the Minister in Charge of Muslim Affairs and other persons nominated by Muslim organizations. The *Mufti* also heads the *fatwa* committee. Again, while *fatwa* has many meanings, within MUIS *fatwa* simply means 'religious ruling'. According to MUIS:

> The *Fatwa* Committee consists of the *Mufti* of Singapore who acts as Chairman of the committee, two members appointed from the MUIS Council and 2 others who are not members of the council. The committee also includes other associate members and resource persons who help to provide relevant inputs before the issue of any religious ruling. Unlike religious queries, *fatwa* refers to questions on emerging issues or issues which do not have clear rulings stated in the *Qur'an* and the Traditions of Prophet Muhammad (peace be upon him).
>
> The *Fatwa* Committee adopts the tenets of the *Shafi'i* school of law. If the following of the tenets of the *Shafi'i* school of law is contrary to the public interest, the *Fatwa* Committee may follow the tenets of any of the other accepted schools of Muslim law as may be considered appropriate. In any case where the ruling is requested in relation to the tenets of a particular school of Muslim law, the *Fatwa* Committee will give its ruling or opinion in accordance with the tenets of that particular school of Muslim law.
>
> (http://www.muis.gov.sg/cms/services/guidance.aspx?id=226)

Under this arrangement, although the state claims that the creation of MUIS allows the needs of the Muslims to be served, it is equally true that MUIS also allows the state to manage the religion of Islam within Singapore.

The next most important aspect of the AMLA is that for Singaporean Muslims, in certain aspects of life, they will come under common law, while for religious matters they will be referred to the *Syariah* courts.

> Apart from the Common Law and Equity, the *Syariah* Court also administers Muslim law in specific personal legal matters governing marriages, divorces, the nullity of marriages and judicial separations under the Administration of Muslim Law Act (AMLA) (1999 Rev Ed) in respect of Muslims or parties married under Muslim law (though the High Court has concurrent jurisdiction with the *Syariah* Court on specific matters relating to maintenance, custody and division of property). Significantly, with respect to issues of inheritance and succession, the AMLA expressly accepts particular Islamic texts as proof of Muslim law.
>
> (Singapore Academy of Law website,
> http://www.singaporelaw.sg/content/LegalSyst1.html)

Interestingly, Singapore's definition of *Syariah* is clearly 'limited' as it really only deals with the registry of Muslims marriages, divorces, inheritances and several other familial matters, and not the broader definition of *Syariah* which in some cases is seen as the only law in a society.

It could be argued that Muslims are 'privileged', in the sense that the state takes such a keen interest in providing for the religious needs of the community. Indeed, the state believes that recognizing Islam and the Muslim community is a key pillar in its ideology and policy of 'multiracialism'. However, the state was completely caught off guard, and unsure of how to react, to the growing significance of Islam within the lives of ordinary Singapore Muslims with the religious resurgence that has taken place in the 1990s.

The Malay-Muslim problem

Ironically, the Malay community in Singapore did indeed modernize, albeit not in the manner that the government foresaw and would have encouraged. Instead of becoming highly rational and utilitarian citizens, the Malay community embraced one important facet of modernization: religiosity. This development in turn created a new problem, which is now known in Singapore as the 'Malay-Muslim problem'. The second half of this chapter is devoted to describing and explaining the shift from what was essentially an 'ethnic' problem to a 'religious' problem.

Although it is impossible to prove definitively, Muslims – as a social group – in Singapore are generally more likely to be 'deeply religious' than any other group. Many other observers – including Suzaina Kadir (2004), Hussin Mutalib (2005) and Noor Aisha Abdul Rahman (2006) – have commented on the fact that Muslims in Singapore are deeply religious, or acknowledge that there has been increasing religiosity, even though none of them have any hard empirical proof of this trend, and they also have not provided any reasons to explain this increasing religiosity. There are, however, some indirect indicators. Using data from the World Values Survey (Singapore) of 2002, we find that Muslims were much more likely to say that religion was 'very important' in their everyday lives, compared to any other group (Table 3.3).

Muslims were also much more likely to select a higher value, on a scale of 1 to 10 with 1 being the least and 10 being the most, that 'God was important' in their lives, compared to other groups, and, with the standard deviation of 0.814, it also meant that Muslims were much more uniform in their views (Table 3.4).

Also, based on another indicator from the World Values Survey (Singapore), Muslims were significantly much more likely to select 'religious faith' – from a list containing views such as 'independence', 'hard work', 'responsibility', 'imagination', 'tolerance', 'thrift', 'determination', 'religious faith', 'unselfishness' and 'obedience' – as something important that should be imparted to the young, at 82 per cent, than any other group (Table 3.5).

Lastly, Muslims were more likely to indicate that they found 'comfort and strength' from religion, when compared to any other group (Table 3.6).

Table 3.3 Importance of religion by religious affiliation

Religion		Per cent
No religion	Very important	5.8
	Rather important	28.8
	Not very important	47.7
	Not at all important	17.7
	Total	100.0
Roman Catholic	Very important	44.8
	Rather important	39.2
	Not very important	9.8
	Not at all important	5.5
	Don't know	0.7
	Total	100.0
Protestant	Very important	72.5
	Rather important	20.1
	Not very important	6.2
	Not at all important	1.2
	Total	100.0
Taoist	Very important	12.9
	Rather important	59.7
	Not very important	21.0
	Not at all important	6.5
	Total	100.0
Chinese religion (Shenism)	Very important	5.7
	Rather important	68.6
	Not very important	20.0
	Not at all important	5.7
	Total	100.0
Muslim	Very important	95.1
	Rather important	4.0
	Not very important	0.7
	Not at all important	0.2
	Total	100.0
Hindu	Very important	65.2
	Rather important	22.5
	Not very important	10.2
	Not at all important	1.7
	Don't know	0.4
	Total	100.0
Buddhist	Very important	17.2
	Rather important	50.4
	Not very important	26.9
	Not at all important	5.5
	Total	100.0
Other religions	Very important	30.9
	Rather important	27.3
	Not very important	29.1
	Not at all important	12.7
	Total	100.0

Source: World Values Survey (Singapore), 2002

Table 3.4 Importance of God(s) in life

Religion	Mean	Std deviation
Muslim	9.85	0.814
Hindu	9.03	1.894
Protestant	8.99	1.678
Roman Catholic	8.20	1.792
Other religions	7.17	3.039
Taoist	6.55	1.889
Buddhist	6.31	2.136
Chinese Religion (Shenism)	6.26	1.709
No religion	5.91	10.806

Source: World Values Survey (Singapore), 2002

Table 3.5 Importance of imparting religious faith to the young

Religion	Valid per cent
Muslim	82.0
Protestant	51.8
Hindu	34.5
Roman Catholic	33.6
Other religions	25.4
Buddhist	16.4
Taoist	16.1
No religion	7.0
Chinese religion (Shenism)	5.7

Source: World Values Survey (Singapore), 2002

Table 3.6 Finding comfort and strength from religion, by religion

Religion	Valid per cent
Muslim	98.4
Protestant	94.6
Roman Catholic	94.2
Hindu	89.8
Other religions	85.4
Buddhist	72.7
Taoist	71.0
Chinese religion (Shenism)	65.7
No religion	32.7

Source: World Values Survey (Singapore), 2002

While most Singaporeans are somewhat 'religious', what could be the reasons behind the very high levels of religiosity amongst the Muslims? We propose that there are three reasons: local, regional and global.

Locally, Singapore is generally a religious society, as shown in the World Values Survey, with more than two-thirds of the population indicating that they consider religion important, and with people with 'no religion' only constituting around 14 per cent. Pereira (2005) proposed that one reason why the overall level of religiosity in Singapore was high may be a consequence of the state's cultural preservation strategy. As part of the Singapore government's ideology of multiracialism, the state openly encouraged and supported the preservation of each ethnic group's identity. Already, in chapter one, we mentioned that the state had in place a 'mother tongue' policy in all schools. Outside of the educational sector, the state's cultural preservation strategy also saw it fund programmes such as the 'Speak Mandarin Campaign' to encourage the Chinese community to retain their linguistic heritage, as well as initiatives like the Malay Cultural Festival Month and the Indian Arts Festival. The reason why the government implemented this strategy was ostensibly to retain Singapore's 'Asian Values', and not to allow Singaporeans to succumb wholly to 'westernization' (Vasil, 2000). As a result, Pereira (2005) argues that as the Chinese were encouraged to celebrate their ethnicity, the Malay community turned to Islam as their main source of ethnic identity.

Another reason why there is high religiosity among Singapore Muslims is that they were influenced by trends in the neighbouring region, especially in the two Muslim-dominated countries closest to Singapore, Malaysia and Indonesia, the latter being the most populous Muslim country in the world. This is due to ongoing social processes such as regional migration and marriage alliances and there remains a significant number of Singaporean Muslims who still have strong familial ties in these two countries and a shared socio-historical background (Djamour, 1965). In both countries, between 1970 and 1990, many observers have noted that there was increasing religiosity among their vast populations. For these countries, modernization and increasing educational attainment had been cited as key factors for the rise in levels of religiosity. Rather than a reaction against modernization, the modernity project – which is inherently contradictory – brought relatively high levels of education to the masses especially among the middle class; this, in turn, led to a re-education of Islam away from the 'folk' Islam to the crystallization of Islamic orthodoxy (Mohamad, 1981: 1040). The re-education – sometimes described as reformism or revivalism – of Islam in the two countries was itself an outcome of globalization (Rinakit and Soesastro, 1998: 194). Two groups from the middle class were the main proponents of this re-education process. The first was the Arabic- and the *madrasah* (Islamic religious schools)-educated group, and the second was made up youths educated in English and Malay. These youths were active in Malaysia and overseas (Shamsul, 2005).

Many non-academic observers believed that fundamentalism would be associated with the uneducated and the rural. Contrary to popular belief, Islam flourished among those who led relatively secure lives such as the middle class. Malay professionals, who included doctors and engineers and many graduate teachers and civil servants, were among those who turned to Islam and decried the secularization of Malay society. This development is illustrated by the fact that *dakwah* (missionary) activities grew rapidly in urban centres like Kuala Lumpur with a large presence of young educated Malays (Nagata, 1984; Shamsul, 2005). Although the situation and context were slightly different in Indonesia, it was found that the *dakwah* movement had become a powerful social movement there as well (Hefner, 2000; Fox, 2004).

Another interesting factor in both Malaysia and Indonesia was the embracing of Islam by the state. In Malaysia, despite various laws, policies, threats and reminders that constrain public discourse on religion and race because they are deemed sensitive matters, the government continued to intensify its Islamization programme (Mauzy and Milne, 1986). In addition, opposition parties such as the *Parti Islam Se-Malaysia* (PAS) have been overtly Islamic in their political platform. This fact, in turn, might have led the ruling United Malays National Organization (UMNO) party to further 'Islamizing' its agenda (Martinez, 2001).

Lastly, Muslims in Singapore have, in addition to these more regional influences, been caught up in the religious revivalism that has swept through the Muslim world in the post-war period, which can be generally described as 'globalizing Islam' (Roy, 2004) or 'resurgent Islam' (Sutton and Vertigans, 2005). Although there are many facets to this renewal, we can briefly summarize the key elements. First, modern transport facilities, especially low-cost, budget airlines, have made it possible for most practising Muslims to aspire to undertake the pilgrimage (the *Hajj*) to the holy cities of Mecca and Medina in their lifetime. Undertaking the *Hajj* confers great status on the participants, but more importantly it exposes them to the wider community and gives the pilgrim a real sense of membership of a global religious movement, namely membership of the Islamic *ummah*. This pattern of pilgrimage has greatly increased the influence of reformist religion in Southeast Asia, where parents are now more likely to want their children to undertake a study of Arabic in order to have a better understanding of the *Qur'an*. In turn there has been a considerable amount of investment from Saudi Arabia in mosques, welfare and education programmes, and funding for pilgrims, thereby increasing the general influence of puritanical Islamic reform movements in the whole of Asia. As people have been caught up in these global changes, there has been a growing consciousness that many of the traditional religious practices of the region are not strictly Islamic. The growing reformism of Islam has expressed itself in a condemnation of age-old syncretism in Southeast Asia. As these influences spread and awareness of Muslim identity deepens, Muslims have become more conscious of the global problems and issues facing Islam such as the conflict with the West that has gone under the banner of the 'war on terror'. Given the easy access to global communications, it is difficult for Singaporean Muslims not to see themselves as connected with the wars involving Muslims in Iraq and Afghanistan, or even the Revolution in Iran.

Second, the revival and renewal movements in Islam can also be understood as aspects of a global competition between the world religions for social and cultural influence, especially in terms of recruiting new members to the faith. The competition between Islam and Christianity in Africa and Asia is particularly significant. Christianity was very quick to adopt modern communication technologies to spread the word of the Gospel. In America, Protestant churches embraced television evangelism as an important strategy to ensure the influence of the Gospel over popular culture, but Christianity also experimented with modern music, text messaging, blog sites and commercialization. The growth of the mega-churches in Asia is a good example of the modernization of Christianity in an effort to influence popular commercial culture, especially among young people. Charismatic mega-churches also have emerged in Singapore among Chinese Christians. Goh (1999) examines three such mega-churches commenting that such churches combine the emotive and experiential aspects of Pentecostalism with the teachings and language of fundamentalism. Some of Singapore's mega-churches promulgate an apocalyptic worldview and the separation of believers from unbelievers. These churches also are often authoritarian insofar as they demand attendees and members adhere to purity codes, demonstrate allegiance to church teachings, and participate in cell groups. In her case study of City Harvest Church, Joy Kooi Chin Tong (2008) shows how the church wields psychological techniques to train and discipline members in order to help individuals overcome the loss of identity in the modern city. In Southeast Asia, some Muslim communities have begun to adopt similar practices of evangelism in their competition with Christianity and in China and Vietnam, with the decline of communism and the emergence of a more liberal regime, religious competition has also intensified (Taylor, 2007). The consequences of these global struggles for cultural influence have again intensified the sense of belonging to a dynamic community that is shaping modern society.

September 11 and after

Before 1990, the stereotypical image of the Malay-Muslim was that he or she was 'backward', hence unable to integrate with the rest of Singaporean society. However, after 1990, with many Muslims embracing the new piety, a different problem of integration emerged. While not often publicly articulated, there were several government leaders that believed that pious Muslims were socially distancing themselves from public life, ostensibly to maintain their religiosity. It took the tragic events from the other side of the world for the Singapore state formally to announce that Muslims in Singapore were a 'social problem'.

On 11 September 2001, the World Trade Center suffered a devastating attack from a radical Muslim group known as Al-Qaeda. Globally, the Muslim population was under suspicion for being, if not complicit, then sympathetic to the terrorist attacks seeking to bring down Western civilization (Huntington, 1993 and 1996; Kepel, 2002). Soon after, the so-called 'war on terror' began under the leadership of the government of the United States of America. In Singapore, 'an unnamed informant' reported that Muhammad Aslam Yar Ali Khan had claimed to have links with Al-Qaeda. As he was about to be placed under surveillance by the Singapore authorities, Muhammad Aslam fled to Pakistan. However, in December 2001, the American troops searching Afghanistan for Al-Qaeda militants arrested Muhammad Aslam. The information provided by Muhammad Aslam ultimately became known in Singapore as the *Jemaah Islamiyah* (JI) Plot (Bilveer Singh, 2007).

The JI Plot included detailed plans on possible terrorist attacks on American installations, including the Embassy of the USA within Singapore. In a video tape found in Afghanistan, there was home-made video footage of several installations as well as certain areas near American installations – such as a Mass Rapid Transit station – which carried narration describing how to attack them. On 9 December 2001, the Singapore authorities, acting on information from Afghanistan, began what became known as the JI arrests. Eventually, 15 more Singaporeans were arrested and placed under the Internal Security Act (ISA), which confers on the government the right to arrest and detain individuals indefinitely without trial.

In October 2002, there were three explosions in the tourist district of Kuta on the Indonesian island of Bali. Two detonated in or near popular tourist nightclubs in Kuta, killing 202 people, 164 of whom were foreign nationals, and 38 Indonesian citizens. A further 209 people were injured. A third smaller device detonated outside the United States consulate in Denpasar, causing only minor damage to property. Various members of the Indonesian chapter of the *Jemaah Islamiyah* were arrested soon after for the 'Bali Bombings'.

The high-profile nature of the attacks on the World Trade Center of 11 September 2001 along with the Bali Bombings of 2002 and the arrests of JI operatives in Singapore provided dramatic evidence for what was known previously to only a few academics, that there was a transnational Islamist movement in Asia that was dedicated to bringing about an Islamic state by violent means if necessary (Gunaratna, 2006). The Southeast Asian component, it was revealed, sought to Islamicize areas from southern Thailand (where there has been conflict between the Muslims and the Thai state), southern Philippines, Malaysia, Singapore and Indonesia.

In January 2003, the Singapore government eventually published a White Paper entitled *The Jemaah Islamiyah Arrests and the Threat of Terrorism* (Singapore Ministry of Home Affairs, 2003) to be presented to Parliament. The function of this White Paper was to use information gathered from the 31 Singaporean JI detainees to outline the following:

> To survey the various self-proclaimed Islamic terrorist groups in Southeast Asia, and to describe the web of relationships that link them together; to delve specifically into the JI and its ties with Al-Qaeda and other radical militant groups; to describe the development of the JI in Singapore, its main terrorist plans here, and the motivations of its members; to outline the report and recommendations of the Internal Security Act Advisory Board that met to consider the case of the JI detainees; and to look ahead to consider how Singapore may protect its people from the threat of terrorism.
>
> (Singapore Ministry of Home Affairs, 2003: 1)

The White Paper reported that psychologists found that of these JI detainees 29 had average or above average intelligence, with two having superior levels of intelligence. They were '... not ignorant, destitute or disenfranchised outcasts. All 31 had received secular education ... like many of their counterparts in militant Islamic organisations in the region, they held normal respectable jobs' (Ministry of Home Affairs, 2003: 15). The White Paper also reported that:

> As a group, most of the detainees regarded religion as their most important personal value. The second highest value they were concerned with was

economic, i.e. having material comforts and material wealth. Spiritual and economic values were followed by social values, such as concern for the well-being of others and being good Muslims to help the *ummah* (Muslim community).

(Singapore Ministry of Home Affairs, 2003: 15)

The White Paper further reported that the psychologists examining the detainees found that:

> Many members turned to leaders like Ibrahim Maidin as they wanted a 'no fuss' path to heaven. They wanted to be convinced that in JI they had found 'true Islam' and free themselves from endless searching as they found it stressful to be critical, evaluative and rational. They believed they could not go wrong, as the JI leaders had quoted from holy texts. The psychological profile of the JI members (e.g. the high compliance, low assertiveness, low in the questioning of religious values, and high levels of guilt and loneliness) suggested that the group of JI members was psychologically pre-disposed to indoctrination and control by the JI leaders and needed a sense of belonging without close attachments. Some were altruistic and wanted to help the *ummah*. Others wanted to accumulate 'points' for a place in heaven.

(Singapore Ministry of Home Affairs, 2003: 17)

The White Paper continued by reporting more conclusions drawn by psychologists who examined the detainees:

> Essentially, the 31 detainees saw no contradiction between living in a prosperous and harmonious multi-racial society and serving in a militant group, be it the JI or the MILF [Moro Islamic Liberation Front]. Although they knew that their actions would harm Singaporeans, they felt that this was an unavoidable price to pay for the advancement of their *jihad*.

(Singapore Ministry of Home Affairs, 2003: 17)

Islamophobia

The attacks by terrorist groups in New York City and Bali, along with the arrests of members of a potential terrorist group in Singapore, transformed the 'Malay-Muslim problem' in Singapore. From a minor worry that Muslims were socially distancing themselves from public life in Singapore because of their high levels of religiosity, there was now a moral panic because Muslims were being stereotyped as terrorists. After the September 11 attacks and the first JI arrests, some Singaporean Muslims felt that they were being treated 'differently'. In a *Singapore Straits Times* article entitled, 'Treated Differently Now, Say Some Muslims', (6 April 2002) a 20-year-old student interviewed observed that 'non-Muslims do treat us differently as they think we are all one'. Voicing their inability to control external events, this student said that '[w]e too are angry at what happened' but asserted that it was unfair to 'judge us [Muslims] as one'. In the same article, a male Indian

Muslim, aged 37, claimed that he was at the receiving end of several 'immature and insensitive remarks'. The article seemed to suggest that non-Muslims had no understanding of Islam. Muslims interviewed in the article felt upset that after 9/11, as it became commonly known, Islam has been under attack with some viewing the religion as 'insular', 'backward', 'anti-progressive' and 'heavy-handed' owing to various practices such as dietary restrictions, daily prayers and yearly fasting.

In another article in the *Singapore Straits Times*, entitled 'Code Red? Code Green? Code Orange!' (16 October 2002), it was reported that the state was very worried about the social strain brought about by the events of 9/11 and the JI arrests. The then-Prime Minister, Goh Chok Tong, reminded non-Muslims that they have to be aware of the way their individual actions could impact the larger society. He warned that if non-Muslims let 'unfounded suspicion affect the way they [non-Muslims] behave towards Muslim Singaporeans, this will build up resentment among Muslims, and turn even the moderate ones against the society'. Instead, Goh advised non-Muslims to rein in their emotions and fear, and urged them to 'act rationally'. Goh then added that 'Muslim Singaporeans must play their part' and warned them against becoming 'exclusive and different'. His point was that if Muslims retreated from public life, it would reduce interaction with the larger society hence increasing distrust. This theme was followed up in January 2003, by a Member of Parliament, Sin Boon Ann, who, in a parliamentary speech, urged Muslims not to set themselves apart:

> Like others elsewhere, Muslims in Singapore are swept up by the tide of Islamic fundamentalism and some are retreating into their own comfort zones.
>
> They are adhering to a certain interpretation of Islam that also gives rise to Islamic militancy.
>
> This was the thrust of Mr Sin Boon Ann's (Tampines GRC) speech in Parliament yesterday.
>
> Describing Islamic fundamentalism as the potent 'political and religious mix of Islam', he noted that while it had its origins in the Middle East, the phenomenon had taken hold in South-east Asia to such an extent that no serious political contender in Malaysia or Indonesia, for example, could afford to ignore the Muslim ground.
>
> Not mincing his words, he said that in Singapore, increasing Islamic fundamentalism has translated into more and more Muslim women donning the *tudung*, and more parents sending their children to madrasahs.
>
> This has in turn led to more Muslims 'retreating into the comfort zones of the mosques for their religious and other needs', he added.
>
> For the sake of strengthening social cohesion, he called upon Muslims not to set themselves apart from the rest of Singapore, but step up their low participation rate in community and grassroots events.
>
> While Mr Sin stressed that he was not against fundamentalism or conservatism, he objected against 'the insistence on one's right to practise and observe his beliefs, even if it means the others may feel that their personal or common public spaces may be encroached or imposed upon'.

Some Muslims here, he noted, have been 'pushing their bounds' by insisting on their religious dress code in schools, referring to cases of parents who have sent their daughters to national schools, wearing the *tudung*.

(*Singapore Straits Times*, 21 January 2003)

The Muslim community soon found itself on the defensive. The Minister in Charge of Muslim Affairs, Yaacob Ibrahim, had to defend Islam by seeking the understanding of the non-Muslims on the issue of communal worship being an integral part of Muslim lives, dispelling worries that Muslims were 'retreating to the mosque at the expense of social interaction' (*Singapore Straits Times*, 22 January 2003). The Minister also touched on this subject, when delivering this response in Parliament on the publication of the White Paper:

> The arrests in Singapore of a group plotting violent terror, and with links to other terrorist groups, both regionally and internationally, brought home a chilling reality, which all Singaporeans hitherto could not have imagined: that there are Singaporeans who are prepared to sacrifice innocent lives for their cause. For the Muslim community in Singapore this is an entirely new phenomenon – the group's total disdain for the sanctity of human life is totally unfamiliar to the community. Nonetheless this new phenomenon brought undue attention to the Muslim community here in Singapore. For the non-Muslim community, it was a test of their trust and faith in fellow Muslim Singaporeans ...
>
> The Malay/Muslim community and religious leaders are united in their determination to tackle these challenges. The responses of the various Malay/Muslim organisations such as MUIS and Mendaki, *Pergas*, *Perdaus* and various community leaders to the White Paper again underscore this commitment. We want to play a constructive role in this important effort of building trust and strengthening ties across all groups in Singapore.
>
> It is also important for the House to know that the Malay/Muslim community had embarked on this process long before the appearance of the White Paper. During the past 2 years or so, Muslim community leaders and institutions have come together to work on measures that will strengthen Islamic religious education and development in Singapore. The Muslim Religious Council of Singapore or MUIS has initiated a variety of programmes to strengthen both the full-time and part-time *madrasah* systems, and to train and upgrade the skills of Islamic religious clerics in Singapore so that they understand the context in which they operate. MUIS has also sought to organise public seminars for both the public and community leaders on issues of importance, and to invite non-Muslim Singaporeans to visit our mosques. MUIS has formed a committee with other Malay/Muslim organisations to study ways to improve the training of local clerics. These are but a few examples of the efforts that are already underway within the Malay/Muslim community.
>
> (Singapore government press release (excerpt), downloaded from http://app-stg.nscc.gov.sg/data/documents/192003_01_21_JIARRESTS_YAACOBSPEECH.doc (accessed 27 July 2008))

There were also other reports in the media that some Muslims were working very hard to change perceptions about the community. For example, the same article cited the case of a mosque Chairman, Suratman Hussein, who used to sit at the 'Muslim table' away from the non-Muslims at public dinners. Such seating arrangements had become the norm because it was easier for catering companies to separate *halal* from non-*halal* food. However, the article reported that Mr Suratman has consciously chosen to dine at the same table with non-Muslims during National Day dinners. He said that '… the message was clear enough … [w]e [Muslims] all have to make that extra effort to reach out' (*Singapore Straits Times*, 13 December 2003).

MUIS also found itself under pressure. In the same article, the President of MUIS revealed that Muslims were '… on their toes now and have become wary of any teaching that might deviate from the norm and even more so if it espouses violence'. He added that Muslims were not '… less psychologically predisposed to indoctrination' by deviationist teachings (*Singapore Straits Times*, 13 December 2003). Since then MUIS has set up an online directory of more than 350 qualified Islamic teachers and the organization and mosques have received queries from members of the public about teachers from whom they are planning to take lessons. The objective of this exercise was ostensibly to 'police' the teaching of Islam in Singapore.

Similarly, Mendaki has called on the critical mass of religious scholars to be at the forefront of the ideological battle against terrorism. In a statement released in response to the release of the White Paper, Mendaki urged the Muslim community to be pro-active in this battle against terrorism to '… ensure that the honour and sanctity of Islam is protected and the religion continues to be a source of progressive inspiration' (*Channel News Asia*, 12 January 2003).

New problem, old problem

The state has generally viewed the Malay-Muslim community as being a problematic, deviant and marginalized minority group in Singapore. Previously, it was suggested that their failure to integrate was due to their inability or refusal to embrace modernization and industrialization. After September 11 the Malay-Muslim community was still criticized for being apart. According to the state, the reason for their distance was their high levels of religiosity. However, if the Muslims were really distancing themselves from the rest of Singaporean society, were they doing this of their own volition, or were being transformed into a social enclave by the state? In the following three chapters, we examined aspects which are very central to religious life for Muslims – dining, education and veiling – to examine if there really was social distancing and enclavement taking place.

4 Social distancing

Halal consciousness and public dining

Introduction: The social distance project

To understand the relationship between individual piety and social distancing, we formulated the 'Social Distance Project'. The literature suggested that the greater the piety of the individual, the more likely he or she would prefer to keep a safe distance from the religiously impure for fear of contamination. Given that contemporary Singapore is modern, secular and multicultural, there would be some aspects of public life which would be deemed to be religiously impure by the pious. These would include public dining establishments, public schools and even interpersonal relations with, for lack of a better term, non-believers. Public dining establishments might contain elements which would be perfectly acceptable to some religions but at the same time prohibited by other religions. Public schools, as they are completely secular, might not provide a proper religious environment for the student. And finally, interpersonal relations, which might include dating and marriage, with non-believers or people of other religions might again conflict with the teachings of the religion and be viewed as being impure. If public dining, attending public schools and interacting with non-believers might threaten religious purity for pious individuals, then it might follow that these individuals would choose to avoid such situations altogether. Thus, piety could possibly lead to social distancing, where the individual intentionally seeks to be apart from the impure. As we have suggested in the opening chapter of this book, if individuals choose to remain apart from the rest of society that is multicultural and secular, then a situation of enclavement might take place, where groups of people do not socially interact with other groups. This in turn would create Furnivall's archetypal 'plural society' (1956), where groups only have economic ties within the marketplace but no social relations with each other. Worse still would be a situation when groups have no contact with each other, not even economic, resulting in a situation of separate ghettoes. Ultimately, plural societies are more likely to be threatened by social instability and inter-group conflict, because the distance between the groups would be more likely to lead to competition and suspicion rather than trust and understanding.

We conceptualized the Social Distance Project to understand whether pious Muslims in contemporary Singaporean society were socially distancing themselves from the rest of multicultural and secular society as a strategy to maintain religious purity. We chose to examine three important acts of piety that might potentially 'conflict' with public life, and as a result might encourage the pious Muslim individual to distance himself or herself: public dining, public schooling and interpersonal relationships with non-Muslims. Other aspects of public life, such as the workplace and public housing, were less feasible sites of study. For the workplace, even within Furnivall's conceptualization of the plural society, individuals can interact freely because the relationships formed are only economic and instrumental. For public housing, while this arrangement could be a powerful site for studying distancing – for example, in some other societies, individuals use segregation of neighbourhoods as the ultimate tool for distancing themselves from groups with whom they do not want to associate – in Singapore this is not possible. This is because the Singapore state has a housing policy – known as the Ethnic Integration Policy – that legislates that the ethnic composition of all public housing estates must reflect the national ethnic ratios (which are 75 per cent Chinese, 15 per cent Malay, and 10 per cent Indian and others) (see Hill and Lian, 1995). Given that over 90 per cent of Singaporeans reside in public housing estates, there is little scope for organizing ethnic or religious segregation spatially.

The Social Distance Project was designed in 2006 to understand how pious Muslims perform or practise acts of piety in public life. Towards this end, we chose to interview 30 'middle class' and self-described pious Muslims. The logic for activating the notion of 'middle class' was chosen in part because of the ways in which the term is commonly used in Singapore. Here, 'middle class' is often accepted as a shorthand for people who have relatively high levels of education (all the respondents in this 'middle class' category had received at least a degree or diploma from a tertiary institution), remuneration and status, and are often employed in white-collar jobs (see Tan, 2004). We felt that the educational attainment of the middle-class person would allow him or her to be more reflective and articulate about his or her attitudes and ideas on various issues. We also sought to have an equal number of male and female respondents. The sample was initially drawn from personal contacts, and complemented by a few referrals. In addition to the 30 middle-class pious Muslims, we also decided to interview ten working-class pious Muslims to see if they held different views on piety and social distancing. Although the highest educational attainments of these ten respondents were primary or secondary school qualifications, in the end we found that there was very little difference in their views on religious issues.

In addition to collecting basic socio-economic and non-identifiable personal information, the interview was primarily designed to elicit views on the three acts of piety: dining in public, public versus religious schools, and interpersonal relations with non-Muslims. The interview utilized broad and general open-ended questions that allowed the respondent to reflect and respond. For the majority of the 40 respondents, the interview lasted an average of 90 minutes. Some of the interviews were conducted separately by the authors (Kamaludeen and Pereira), while the rest were conducted by a hired research assistant. The interviews began in June 2007 with the final interview being concluded in June 2008.

Halal as social distancing

> Bassanio: If it please you to dine with us.
> Shylock: Yes, to smell pork, to eat of the habitation which your prophet the
> Nazarite conjured the devil into. I will buy with you, sell with you, talk
> with you, walk with you and so following. But I will not eat with you,
> drink with you, nor pray with you.
>
> Shakespeare: *The Merchant of Venice* (Act 1 Scene 3: 27–32)

In this scene, the character Shylock is a Jewish merchant who declines to dine with Bassanio because of his religious beliefs. Like Judaism, Islam has explicitly clear rules indicating the types of food and drinks that are permissible for consumption (*halal*) and others which are prohibited (*haram*).

> The basic guidance about the *halal* food laws is revealed in the *Qur'an* (the divine book) from God (the Creator) to Muhammad (the Prophet) for all people. The food laws are explained and put into practice through the *Sunnah* (the life, actions, and teachings of Muhammad) as recorded in the *Hadith* (the compilation of the traditions of Muhammad). In general, everything is permitted for human use and benefit. Nothing is forbidden except what is prohibited either by a verse of the *Qur'an* or an authentic and explicit *Sunnah* of Muhammad. These rules of *Shariah* (Islamic Law) bring freedom for people to eat and drink anything they like as long as it is not *haram* (prohibited).
>
> (Riaz and Chaudry, 2004: 1)

In this sense, that Islam has certain food and drink prohibitions is not unusual. Many other religions also have similar restrictions, including *kosher* rules for Jews, and beef prohibitions for Hindus for example. Furthermore, some Buddhists believe that eating meat altogether is not permissible; hence, they are vegetarians. In Islam, all food and drink are clearly divided into *halal* (permissible) and *haram* (prohibited). For Islam, the *Qur'an* clearly specifies food and drink that are considered *haram*, and various verses also offer explanations for these prohibitions. In essence, all food is permitted for consumption by the Muslims, except the following categories, including any products derived from them or contaminated with them. These are summarized as:

- Carrion or dead animals
- Swine (all variants), including all by-products
- Animals slaughtered without pronouncing the name of God on them
- Animals killed in a manner that prevents their blood from being fully drained from their bodies
- Animals slaughtered while pronouncing a name other than God
- Intoxicants of all types, including alcohol and drugs
- Carnivorous animals with fangs, such as lions, dogs, wolves or tigers
- Birds with sharp claws (birds of prey), such as falcons, eagles, owls, or vultures
- Such creatures as frogs or snakes

(Riaz and Chaudry, 2004: 15)

With regards to prohibited drink, Yusuf Al Qaradawi has stated that Muslims are ordered to stay away from drinking parties or gatherings at which alcoholic drinks are served, stating that it was the duty of a Muslim to eradicate any evil he or she encounters. In the event Muslims are not able to do so, they must stay away from such gatherings and leave behind those who are engaged in such harmful practices. He underlined his point by citing the *hadith* (or tradition) of the Prophet Muhammad, 'Whoever believes in Allah and the Last Day must not sit at table at which *khamr* is consumed' (Al-Qaradawi, 1994: 74). Al-Qaradawi defines *khamr* as 'any substance which intoxicates, in whatever form or under whatever name it may appear. Thus, for example, beer and similar drinks are *haram*' (Al-Qaradawi, 1994: 71–2).

From a theological perspective, Muslims are taught that it is a virtue to only consume *halal* food. The following translation of a Friday sermon given by MUIS illustrates this by asserting that:

> A good Muslim would pay attention to what he eats, for whatever he put into his mouth would be a part of him, and has an effect not only on his physical body, but also on his spiritual self. And by taking only those that are *halal* and good, a good Muslim is showing his gratitude towards Allah for all the blessings Allah has given.
>
> (MUIS, 1 June 2007)

In addition, MUIS explains why alcohol is prohibited by Islamic law:

> Alcoholic drinks too have proved to be dangerous to ourselves. On top of impairing our mind, it brings us physical illness like high blood pressure, as well as many social illnesses, for a person who is drunk will most likely be destructive.
>
> (MUIS, 1 June 2007)

It is also important to note that under Islamic law, not only are there rules and prohibitions regarding food and drink, but the slaughtering, processing and serving of any food and drink must also conform to Islamic law. For example, with regards to the slaughtering of animals, the animal must be of a *halal* species. The animal must be slaughtered by a Muslim of proper age, the name of God must be pronounced at the time of slaughter, and the slaughter must be done by cutting the throat of the animal in a manner that induces rapid, complete bleeding and results in the quickest death (Riaz and Chaudry, 2004: 18). In addition, the environment where *halal* food is processed must also be completely free from *haram* products.

It is also significant that within the last 50 years, there has been a formalization of the *halal* food and drink process. More specifically, unlike the past where food processing and production had been a traditional and local practice, there are now many international, national and regional organizations that issue *halal* certificates (Riaz and Chaudry, 2004: 78). This has allowed the import and export of *halal*-certified food, as will be discussed later. In Singapore, the regulation of *halal* certification is undertaken by MUIS. Its powers are delineated in the AMLA:

- Section 88A(1): The *Majlis* [MUIS] may issue *halal* certificates in relation to any product, service or activity and regulate the holders of such certificates to ensure that the requirements of the Muslim law are complied with in the production, processing, marketing or display of that product, the provision of that service or the carrying out of that activity
- Section 88A(5): Any person who, without the approval of the *Majlis* a) issues a *halal* certificate in relation to any product, service or activity; or b) uses any specified *halal* certification mark or any colourable imitation thereof, shall be guilty of an offence and shall be liable on conviction to a fine not exceeding $10,000 or to imprisonment for a term not exceeding 12 months or both

MUIS has been issuing *halal* certificates since 1978 for the following establishments: restaurants, stalls within a school canteen, snackbars, *Halal* corners (food stands), confectioneries, bakery shops and stalls within a food court or its equivalent. According to the MUIS *Halal* Certification Terms and Conditions (2008), the certification process involves four mandatory stages: application, certification, certification audit and post-certification (http://www.muis.gov.sg/cms/services/hal.aspx?id=85). In the application stage, the applicant must prepare documents specifying all the products to be used in the preparation of food and drinks, including declaration letters from food suppliers and/or laboratory analysis reports:

> An analysis report from any accredited laboratories may be required upon notice by MUIS to confirm that the food does NOT contain non-*Halal* raw materials, for instance, animals, animal derivatives and ethanol. The food sample(s) for testing must be taken by the above test agency personally or by MUIS personnel from the applicant's premises and sealed with the *Muis* security seal. The applicant is to bear all costs of the laboratory testing.
>
> (Item 2.2.3 of MUIS *Halal* Certification Terms and Conditions;
> http://www.muis.gov.sg/cms/services/hal.aspx?id=85)

At the Certification stage, MUIS requires applicants to declare that:

> All production lines, crockery, kitchen utensils and equipments, cooking place, chillers, freezers, cold rooms, etc. must be ritually cleansed by MUIS appointed personnel if they had been previously used for preparation of pork and pork-related items. All *Halal* food/raw materials must be prepared and stored separately from non-*Halal* food items, and there must be a clear indication to distinguish them. Cross contamination between the equipments/utensils used for *Halal* and non-*Halal* food should be avoided.
>
> (Item 2.2.4-5 of MUIS *Halal* Certification Terms and Conditions;
> http://www.muis.gov.sg/cms/services/ hal.aspx?id=85)

In addition, the applicant must ensure that the '*Halal* team', particularly the Muslim staff and at least one other member, undergo the MUIS *Halal* training programme (Item 2.4.2). After the certification stage is complete, the applying foodstall must begin operation in order that MUIS may audit its practices. While the audit encompasses many items, perhaps the most pertinent is that 'the scope of audit will cover from the delivery of raw materials to the washing of used utensils (including preparation of food, sale of food and collection of utensils)' (Item 3.1.2). If the applying foodstall satisfies the criteria set by MUIS, it will receive approval by way of the MUIS *Halal* Certificate, valid for a specified term. However, that is not the end of the process, as there are several post-certification stages, including 'spot checks' conducted by MUIS to ensure that *halal* practices are maintained at the foodstall, as well as the renewal of the Certificate exercise beyond the original term.

Also, MUIS recognizes certain international, national and regional *halal* certification centres based in other countries. This allows approved *halal* products to be imported into Singapore, which typically does not produce or grow food of its own due to its small land size. Finally, MUIS also certifies Singaporean entrepreneurs to export their products to a global *halal* market, as well as certifies local establishments (such as restaurants, food courts and individual stalls) as being compliant with religious regulations.

Overall, it is evident that observing *halal* practices is important for interested organizations, such as MUIS and food vendors. However, is *halal* in actuality important to Muslims? In theory, there are no sanctions that can be imposed on Muslims if they do not adhere to *halal* practices. We therefore wanted to understand if observing *halal*-ness was important to Muslims in Singapore. If practising and pious Muslims adhere to these rules, we suggest they would have a '*halal* consciousness' which defines the habitus of pious persons. However, would piety affect a Muslim's participation in everyday life in a secular and multicultural society, which might not be *halal*? Would the individual choose to distance himself or herself, or perhaps altogether avoid, non-*halal* environments? These questions are important, not only because there is a high degree of religiosity or piety among Muslims in Singapore, but also because most of Singapore's public life is generally tailored for the dominant population, who are not Muslims.

Public dining in multicultural Singapore

> Eating and drinking, the oldest and intellectually most negligible functions, can form a tie, often the only one, among very heterogeneous persons and groups.
>
> Georg Simmel (1950: 33)

Singapore's small geographical size, high population density, urbanization and racial diversity have influenced the state's policymaking process in a number of ways. First, the Singapore state has had in place a policy of multiracialism since national independence in 1965. Of the many facets of multiracialism, three are relevant here. The first is a policy of social integration. Because there were inter-racial conflicts during Singapore's pre-independence era, the state implemented a series of measures to foster racial harmony in Singapore. These include ensuring that most aspects of public life in Singapore are 'multiracial'. For example, we have already mentioned that the state has legislated that all public housing estates must conform to the racial ratios of Singaporean society. This practice of having proportional ethnic representation is also present in the education system, where ethnic ratios are also enforced in most primary and secondary schools. The logic behind this initiative is to ensure that there is inter-ethnic interaction, which is believed by the state to improve racial harmony. To reiterate, for the Singapore state cultural diversity is not just a fact of life, but a desired outcome.

Second, the state has invested heavily in the construction of many public or 'satellite' housing estates situated across the island, where Singaporeans can gain access to low-cost public housing. In 2001, over 90 per cent of Singapore's resident population resided in public housing estates. Given that the state has strict racial quotas for these estates, there are no palpable ethnic enclaves in Singapore and even in the highly popular areas known as Chinatown, Little India and Geylang Serai (Malay area) there are in fact no resident ethnic enclaves, but only cultural constructions for tourism (Chang, 1999). Of relevance to this chapter, in these carefully planned public housing estates, the state has created public spaces – often around main transportation hubs – where much of communal life takes place. This provision of public space also includes commercial, retail and dining outlets. Most of the dining outlets – including restaurants, cafes, food courts, hawker centres, coffee shops and similar establishments – are operated by private enterprises. Interestingly, most food courts and hawker centres also tend to gravitate towards providing food almost in proportion to Singapore's racial and ethnic ratios (see Chua and Rajah, 2003). For example, in a typical 10-stall food court, there will be one *halal* Malay vendor and one Indian food vendor, even though there is no law enforcing the multiracial quotas for food courts. Still, public dining in Singapore is generally multiracial just as much as everyday life is in the society as a whole.

Third, 'dining out' is a popular aspect of daily life in Singapore, especially with what is known as 'low-end dining' as opposed to 'fine' or 'high-end' dining. One reason for this practice is the relative low cost of dining at food courts or hawker centres. Also, the relative abundance of these low-end establishments means that it becomes convenient for most Singaporeans to dine affordably at a food court or hawker centre. It is interesting to note that the Singapore Tourism Board has even embarked on a publicity campaign to highlight the fact that dining in Singapore would not be complete without a visit to a typically Singaporean hawker centre, which will have various ethnic food stalls (see http://www.visitsingapore.com/).

The ritual problem, particularly for a pious and practicing person of any religion, is that multiracial or multicultural public life can be potentially fraught with conflict. For example, in the sphere of public dining, quite literally, one man's meat might be another man's poison. Hence, at a hawker centre, food court or restaurant, beef – which is prohibited by Buddhism – or pork – which is prohibited by Islam – could be sold and consumed by communities that do not have these dietary restrictions. Similarly, alcohol, whose consumption is restricted by certain Christians and by all Muslims, can be readily found at many public establishments. Given that public dining is a regular and much celebrated aspect of ordinary life in multicultural Singapore, there exists the possibility that there can be occasions or situations where the pious Muslim might be faced with food, drink and even practices which are not *halal*. How would he or she cope? Or would he or she choose to avoid the whole situation altogether? In this segment of the Social Distance Project, we asked respondents questions that gave an insight into their *halal* consciousness.

Halal consciousness

> If more and more Muslims demand to see *halal* certificates of the caterers or restaurants before they agree to join non-Muslims for a *makan* (meal), you send the signal of a community that wants to be exclusive. When that happens, the other communities will keep their distance.
>
> (Then-Prime Minister Goh Chok Tong, quoted in
> *Singapore Straits Times*, 3 February 2002)

We found from the interviews that *halal* consciousness among all the respondents was high; in other words, the respondents were constantly on the alert when in public dining establishments – such as hawker centres, restaurants and food courts – to seek out the *halal* and avoid the *haram*. This behaviour was perhaps not surprising, because all the respondents described themselves as being 'very religious'. However, when probed further, all of them mentioned that they would not compromise on *halal*-ness, and would rather forego eating out altogether than eating non-*halal* food. When dining in public, the respondents said that they would only patronize stalls that were *halal*. More specifically, they said that they would actively look out for the MUIS *halal* certificate for assurance. For all of them, they would not patronize a food stall that claimed to have 'no pork, no lard, using only vegetable oil' – this phrase is sometimes used by vendors, who are usually non-Muslims, and who do not have MUIS *halal* certification.

> I have my reservations about chicken wings because some vendors have the tendency to just buy the cheaper one and ignore the *halal*. You'll never know as this is difficult to check.
>
> (Teacher, male, 28)

Implicit in this statement is the perception that non-*halal* certified products generally cost less than *halal*-certified products. This is because the procedures and regulation of *halal* status invokes higher operational costs, as opposed to non-*halal* food production. For instance, some of Singapore's fresh poultry comes from (Chinese) farms in Malaysia that do not have *halal* certification. As such, the respondent was suggesting that it is possible that an unscrupulous vendor who might have a MUIS *halal* certificate might choose to use cheaper non-*halal* chicken. In this situation, trust and perception appear to be very important factors when deciding whether or not to patronize a particular vendor.

Thus, restaurants that have managed to acquire MUIS *halal* certification are very eager to maintain this status, not only because it is a mandatory requirement, but also because it affects the mentality of potential customers.

> Customers are also not allowed to bring outside food to preserve the *halal* status of the food that is served.
>
> (Business Executive of a halal restaurant, male, late 20s)

Despite the certification, the respondents have shown that they are always questioning whether the food and its preparation are actually *halal*.

> It depends on the companies too. If the companies are big, we will trust them. Like McDonald's. My brother saw that the meat from McDonald's have *halal* certification. So they're ok. But some small companies have been prosecuted by MUIS for breaching *halal* regulations.
>
> (Housewife, 52)

> Thinking about it, I even have my doubts about some Muslim vendors [whether they follow *halal* practices]. You have to see how the person is, whether he is sloppily dressed, whether he does things anyhow. If he seems 'dodgy', then I won't buy food from him, even if he is Muslim.
>
> (Teacher, male, 28)

For deeply religious Muslims, their *halal* consciousness keeps them vigilant especially in the light of recent incidents involving two local supermarket chains, Sheng Siong Supermarket Pte Ld and NTUC Fairprice, where the *halal* certificate was apparently abused or wrongly used. In the first case, Sheng Siong Supermarket Pte Ltd was fined S\$600 by the Subordinate Court for misusing the *halal* label after a member of the Muslim community filed a complaint with MUIS, and pictures and news of 'Lucky Instant Noodle with Fried Pork Flavour' made its rounds on the Internet (*Berita Harian*, 14 November 2008). In a separate incident, NTUC Fairprice has filed a police report after a shopper produced a photograph of a packet of NTUC Pasar brand pork coming with a MUIS *halal* sticker. NTUC Fairprice has released a statement stating that their original packaging comes without the *halal* sticker (*Channel News Asia*, 1 November 2007). Even though both cases could have been mistakes or pranks, it suggests that religious Muslims in Singapore consider *halal*-ness paramount, and will take a defensive or sceptical approach towards foodstuffs, regardless of the certification.

To further support this view, one respondent mentioned that she would prefer to frequent restaurants that not only sell *halal* food, but also restaurants whose food is cooked and prepared by Muslims. This is because it is possible for a *halal*-certified establishment to hire non-Muslims as cooks, waiters and cleaners.

> Our Chinese cooks are not allowed to bring or consume any outside food. We have 5 Chinese cooks. 2 are Buddhists and 3 free thinkers. Sometimes our neighbouring shops give out beers, especially during festive seasons, as gifts to our Chinese cooks. We make sure that they send it home immediately. If

people were to see beer bottles lying around in the restaurant we are shooting our own ass. Customers are also not allowed to bring outside food to preserve the *halal* status of the food that is served.

(Manager of a local Muslim Restaurant, male, 20s)

The interviews showed very clearly that the respondents were very concerned about adhering to the *halal* rules. This was further reinforced by the fact that most respondents were continuously scrutinizing the authenticity of *halal* food, especially from vendors that they were unfamiliar with. As our research shows, most of the respondents indicated that 'when in doubt [about the *halal* status of a food], do not proceed'. There was almost no indication that any of the respondents would compromise.

Many non-Muslim caterers, hawkers and restaurateurs have responded to the high level of *halal* consciousness among Muslims by acquiring formal *halal* certification, in order to cater to the Muslim market. As we have indicated in an earlier section, MUIS is solely in charge of the administration of *halal* certification in the country. In 2005, MUIS reported a 27 per cent increase in applications for *halal* certification with the increase coming mainly from the food industry (*Singapore Straits Times*, 5 February 2005). One of the main reasons for this growth, it can be argued, is the increasing religiosity of Singaporean Muslims, as we have shown in the previous chapter (also see Tan, 2004; Mukhlis, 2006) manifesting itself in a greater interest in adherence to Islamic requirements especially relating to diet (Funston, 2006: 75).

Perhaps the most obvious example of this change is the recent emergence of a *halal*-certified food court chain, known as Banquet, which has 13 outlets in Singapore in 2008. Banquet is unique because, unlike other food court chains such as Kopitiam or Food Junction, it ensures that the entire food court is *halal*. Interestingly, Banquet does not simply serve ethnic Malay food. Instead, Banquet attempts to replicate all the usual fare that can be found in the archetypal Singaporean food court or hawker centre, including Chinese, Malay, Indian, European and other (such as Japanese or Korean) cuisine, except that all the ingredients are *halal* certified.

The reasons for Banquet's emergence include not only the high level of *halal* consciousness among Muslims but also the growth of the Malay-Muslim middle class, which now has greater spending power. Banquet also does not lose out, because non-Muslims too are able to consume *halal* food. These reasons probably created a viable business model for Banquet. It is highly likely that this model was first pioneered by the multinational fast-food chains, such as McDonalds' Restaurants, Kentucky Fried Chicken (KFC), Pizza Hut and Burger King, among others. These establishments amended their menus and food production methods to gain official *halal* certification in Singapore permitting them to attract the Muslim market. For example, pork, ham and bacon – found in pizzas and accompanying some burgers – were replaced by *halal* turkey or chicken 'ham' and 'bacon'. Yet, these establishments continued to appeal to the non-Muslim market by essentially not altering their food fare significantly.

Halal environment

> We believe, in any event, that the body obeys the exclusive laws of physiology and that it escapes the influence of history, but this too is false. The body is molded by a great many distinct regimes; it is broken down by the rhythms of work, rest, and holidays; it is poisoned by food or values through eating habits or moral laws; it constructs resistances.
>
> (Foucault, 1977: 153)

As suggested earlier, *halal* consciousness among pious Muslims is high. However, we found that this consciousness is not just restricted to the food or drink themselves but to the surrounding environment as well. This requirement is because pious Muslims believe that *haram* items have the ability to contaminate *halal* food, drink and environment. This notion becomes particularly problematic for devout Muslims dining publicly in a multicultural society, where in a food court or hawker centre, there might be stalls selling *haram* food and drinks, such as pork and alcohol, to non-Muslims.

We asked the respondents if they would willingly choose to exclude themselves from these social environments, where *haram* food and drinks were sold and consumed. Most of the respondents reported that they did not mind eating in a food court or hawker centre so long as there was at least one *halal*-certified vendor. Many said that the presence of non-*halal* and *haram* food and drinks was not a problem, but they obviously would not patronize those vendors. However, in such cases, we found that many embraced 'defensive dining' strategies in mixed food courts or hawker centres.

> I will not place my bare hands on the table whenever I dine at an outlet that serves both *halal* and non-*halal* food. The rag that is used to wipe the table has also been used to clean the other tables [where there might be non-*halal* and *haram* food].
>
> (IT Executive, male, 20s)

When asked about dining together with non-Muslims who might be consuming non-*halal* or *haram* food, many respondents talked about the need to establish 'a safe distance' between friends/colleagues/strangers eating non-*halal* food and themselves. This strategy is so that the '*halal*-ness' (religious purity) of their food can be safeguarded and preserved. If the non-*halal* food were to come within too close a proximity, then the '*halal*-ness' of the Muslims' own food could be threatened owing to accidental or unintentional spilling, splashing and so on.

> Of course as far as possible I wouldn't want to be close but I won't stop them if they want [to sit at the same table]. It's the same with any other condition say for example on a plane, if the person beside you drinks beer, you can't tell him no or to insist on sitting beside a non-alcoholic drinker.
>
> (Airline Station Manager, male, late 20s)

Hence, both respondents reported that they employed 'vigilance', which meant that they were constantly on the look out for situations where 'contamination' might take place.

> When dining with non-Muslims eating at the same table there must be reasonable distance. In Singapore, [it] cannot be avoided, we have to share tables. If they are eating food with soup or a lot of sauce, then I don't want to sit there. If they eat, it will splash all over.
>
> (Businesswoman, female, 40s)

There were other means to dine defensively, including selecting where one sits to have the meal.

> With respect to the seating arrangement when dining in an eatery or hawker centre selling both *halal* and non-*halal* food, I always try to sit at a distance from the stalls selling non-*halal* food. Nearer the *halal* food is better.
>
> (Policy analyst, female, mid 20s)

Many respondents also activated defensive strategies as a means to cope with the unwelcome presence of alcohol nearby.

> If I eat with non-Muslims and they drink beer, in a formal situation like functions then you can't really do anything about it, I'll just tolerate. If it is a private function, I'll ask my friends not to consume alcohol. Even for drinks, I prefer to buy from Muslim stalls because of the washing of cups and all that.
>
> (Teacher, male, 28)

In one part of the interview, we asked respondents when they had to attend a dinner function or a banquet whether they would prefer to be at an all-*halal* table, or whether they would prefer to sit in mixed tables. In Singapore, there have been two positions on this issue: to have separate tables for Muslims (and also separate tables for vegetarians), or to have common tables but individualized servings (hence, the Muslim person at the table would receive a *halal* meal served with different utensils). The responses reflected the dilemma that many pious Muslims faced. Their primary feeling was to prefer to be at a separate table, but they did not want to be apart from their non-Muslim friends. As such, many were willing to compromise by joining a mixed table if they were assured that they would be served individual *halal* food with different utensils. We thus concluded that these pious Muslims showed a willingness to integrate, albeit just to be with their non-Muslims friends.

When it comes to what constitutes a safe and reasonable distance, the issue of the olfactory – also known as 'the aroma of food' – becomes pertinent. Based on the responses in this research, we found that some respondents reject dining at the same table as a non-Muslim who is consuming pork or alcohol on the basis of smell.

If I can smell the pork, I cannot accept because of the smell. Alcohol, as well. Oh, the smell! Even in public transport, I'll move to another seat if someone who consumes alcohol is sitting near me. It's not because I look down on the alcoholics and all. It's just because I have a sensitive sense of smell.

(Businesswoman, 40s)

If possible there must be a distance between the *halal* and non-*halal* stalls. Sometimes the smell is so strong. If it is too close, I don't like it.

(Kitchen Helper in a Muslim Restaurant, female, 50s)

(Translated) Just the smell [of pork] can make my throat go queasy and squeamish.

(Tailor, female, 46)

Some respondents, however, took a more reflexive viewpoint with attempts at citing the Islamic jurisprudence, which has restrictions on contact or consumption but not smell.

The smell of the pork is nothing. Of course it smells bad, but from a religious perspective, it's nothing. I used to eat with my Chinese friend and everyone … Of course it's not that comfortable because of the smell. But while I try to ignore, I still don't feel so comfortable.

(Taxi Driver, male, late 40s)

Hence, we found that the concerns of the respondents go beyond merely consuming *halal* food. Their *halal* consciousness also took into account the social and physical conditions of their surroundings.

Exclusive *halal* zone?

If pious Muslims had such a strong *halal* consciousness, would they prefer a situation where not only would the food be *halal*, but also it would be served in an all-*halal* environment? Most respondents said that it would be much more convenient if the whole environment was *halal*.

Normally, I go for Malay food courts or hawker centres which serve all *halal* food. I do not go to a place where a majority of the stalls serve alcoholic drinks and pork, and there would be only one Indian stall that serves *halal* food. At West Coast, where there are certain separations [between *halal* and non-*halal* stalls], it is ok.

(Taxi Driver, male, late 40s)

Yet, when probed further, nearly all of the respondents said that they – in actual practice – did not exclusively patronize fully *halal* food courts or hawker centres. Instead, all the respondents reported that they would regularly go to a 'mixed' establishment, which would have at least one *halal*-certified vendor, and where they would practise defensive dining. However, was this willingness to patronize a mixed *halal* and non-*halal* establishment the result of a lack of choice – there was only one all-*halal* Banquet food court chain compared to the many other food court chains that were mixed – or was this their own choice? The general view was that patronizing a food court with at least one *halal*-certified stall was acceptable and normal. For example, one respondent even said that he would prefer to eat 'good *halal* food in a mixed environment', than 'bad tasting *halal* food in an all-*halal* food court'.

To explain this view, we proposed that pious Muslims were seeking to be pious and pragmatic at the same time. In other words, while they tried to remain true to the teachings of their religion, they were also pragmatic in accepting that they could achieve their religious expectations with regards to public dining if they took a few additional safeguards. This would allow them a wider choice of public dining establishments than if they were restricting themselves only to total *halal* outlets. Although the number of such establishments has been growing over the recent years, they currently still only form a small proportion when compared to the total number of food courts and hawker centres in Singapore. Thus, it can be concluded that their personal preference for a total *halal* environment is a wish for convenience – where they do not need to be on high defensive alert all the time – rather than exclusivity. Hence, we did not sense that there was a strong demand for all-*halal* dining zones, even among pious Muslims.

In February 2008, in an article entitled 'School's "*halal* zone" ruling causes stir' (*Singapore Straits Times*, 5 February 2008), it was reported that a principal of Boon Lay Primary School, Mr Wan Imran Woojdy, had written to all the parents of students informing them that the school canteen had been certified *halal*, which meant that it would only serve foods and drinks that are permissible according to Islamic laws. While many schools in Singapore have *halal* canteens, this particular school went one step further to insist that students would not be allowed to bring their own non-*halal* food, which might have been packed from home, onto the school premises. To enforce this interpretation of the school's ruling, the school security guard and discipline master had been checking lunch boxes to ensure all pupils complied with the *halal* ruling. Some non-Muslim parents had complained to the newspaper and to the Ministry of Education that it was 'unfair that students could not bring their own non-*halal* foods into the canteen' (*Singapore Straits Times*, 5 February 2008). The article continued:

> When contacted earlier yesterday, principal Imran said the rule forbidding non-*halal* food in the canteen had been in place since 2002, when all eight food stalls were certified *halal* by the Islamic Religious Council of Singapore (MUIS). He said that the school decided to enforce the rule as it had a new canteen contractor and had to get recertified by MUIS. 'We decided to make the whole canteen *halal* to provide a common eating space for all our children, whatever their race', he said.
>
> (*Singapore Straits Times*, 5 February 2008)

The end result was that the state had to step in to defuse the problem. The Ministry of Education decided that the principal was in error and he was not allowed to designate the entire canteen as being *halal*. He had misunderstood the MUIS requirement, because MUIS did not require the whole canteen to be *halal*, but only that the stalls serving food be *halal* (*Singapore Straits Times*, 5 February 2008). In other words, students could bring non-*halal* food and drinks into the canteen.

> When contacted, the MOE [Ministry of Education] said the school had made an error and regretted the concern caused to parents. Its spokesman added: 'Schools will continue to ensure the preservation of common space for all pupils, and educate them on the multiracial and multi-religious nature of Singapore'.
>
> (*Singapore Straits Times*, 5 February 2008)

This episode was interesting because it showed that the principal of this school, a Muslim, was intending to create a space that not only served food which complied with Islamic dietary requirements but also to ensure that prohibited food and drink were kept out in order to eliminate the possibility of contamination. In other words, the principal was attempting to make the school canteen a religiously pure enclave or a 'safe zone'.

Some respondents, who were interviewed after the episode, were asked for their views on such a 'safe zone'. Most of these respondents said that they understood the motivations of the principal, but also understood the state's response.

> It does make sense to have an all-*halal* canteen. After all, the Chinese can eat *halal* food too … but I guess this made the non-Muslims unhappy. I think no need to be so strict [as to completely restrict non-Muslim food from the canteen]. Since all the stalls are *halal*, then the only issue is the non-*halal* brought in by the students. You know children, they are not so careful, might drop food everywhere. But if the Muslim students are careful, they can avoid all these problems. So, in the end, I think no need to have an all-*halal* canteen after all.
>
> (Postgraduate researcher, female, 25)

> I think the principal in question was just a bit too enthusiastic. He wanted to make the canteen like Banquet food court. I agree that it would be good for Muslim children, but it is not good in a school setting. After all, for non-Muslims outside [school], they have a choice of whether to go to Banquet or somewhere else. But in a school canteen, they do not have a choice. Everyone must share the same facilities. So in this case, if there are *halal* stalls, then it is enough.
>
> (Librarian, female, 35)

While we discerned some frustration from some respondents regarding such a 'small matter' – some felt the incident could have been handled more tactfully by the state rather than having it 'splashed all over the front page of the *Straits Times*', or 'making the Muslims sound like they were very demanding' – those who were asked about the incident ultimately felt that the right outcome was achieved. In other words, it was acceptable that all the stalls were *halal* certified, but there was no need for the whole canteen to be *halal* and there ought not to be a ban on home-prepared non-*halal* food brought by students. When added to the rest of the views from the respondents, we would conclude that at least in Singapore there was no strong demand for all-*halal* zones. Pious Muslims seemed to be satisfied with the current situation and they were quite willing to enter into mixed *halal* and non-*halal* zones, as long as they were confident that they could practise 'defensive dining' strategies.

Defensive dining

It is clear that most of the pious Muslims interviewed in this research have a very high level of *halal* consciousness. On the issue of public dining, they indicated that they prefer not to have to engage in defensive dining strategies but would do so when the occasion necessitates. In other words, they would prefer to dine in an environment which is totally *halal*, if there was a choice. Yet, the apparent frequency with which these individuals actually patronize establishments which are not totally *halal*, and when they have to activate defensive dining, either out of necessity if there are no totally *halal* establishments available, or out of choice – for example they want to enjoy the company of non-Muslims on occasions – suggest that they are not exclusionist in principle. In other words, defensive dining indicates participation through a combination of accommodation and negotiation, rather than social separation.

As such, as far as public dining for Singapore's Muslims is concerned, unlike Shakespeare's Shylock, piety does not immediately imply self-exclusion even though there is a growing *halal*-certified market. Instead, we argue that the *halal*-certification scheme – although commercially driven – is in fact an integrating process because it allows even the most devout Muslim, who is supposed to be the most selective about food and drink consumption, to patronize public mixed establishments. At the same time, the all-*halal* establishments, such as the Banquet food courts, do not exclude non-Muslims. State intervention is clearly necessary to maintain the balance between religious groups in civil society and this intervention is fundamental as the case of the school principal's *halal* ruling over school meals decisively illustrates.

5 Religious or public education?

The *madrasah* dilemma

Introduction

In 2004, there were over 1000 applicants vying for 400 places at the *Madrasah* Al-Junied (Suzaina, 2005: 13). This is already an increase over the reported 800 applicants for the same 400 places in 2000 (*Singapore Straits Times,* 3 June 2000). This full-time *madrasah,* which is Malay for Islamic religious school, along with five other similar *madrasahs* in Singapore, had been facing strong demand for places for nearly a decade (*Singapore Straits Times,* 1 March 1998). The logical course of action would be to expand the *madrasah* system to accommodate the growing demand. However, this is not possible in contemporary Singapore. The state maintains that full-time *madrasahs* are solely for the purposes of training Singapore's future Islamic clerics, administrators and scholars. As such, the state has calculated that the enrolment in the six existing *madrasahs* is sufficient to train these specialists each year. All other Muslim children are expected to attend the many schools in the national educational system.

We sought to understand this strong demand for places in Singapore's *madrasahs.* We assumed that, based on the literature on piety and social distancing, this high demand was because pious Muslims not only wanted their children to be educated in Islamic theology but to also be socialized in a proper Islamic rather than in a secular environment. Education, after family socialization, is the most powerful form of social reproduction and since some Muslims parents are very religious, it is to be expected that they would prefer their children to also be pious. Also the full-time *madrasahs* might be perceived by pious Muslims as being run by Muslims and for the Muslim community. For instance, every aspect of the *madrasah* including the structure and organization of the classrooms and dining areas would be in accordance with Islamic requirements. Thus, *madrasahs* can be seen to provide an environment that is much more conducive for Muslim children than public schools, which are meant for students of any or no faith. Based on this logic, we hypothesized that the reason behind this strong demand from Singapore Muslims is that the *madrasah* is valued, over and above its theological function, because it is a religiously safe and pure enclave. This can create two potential sources of conflict. First, the Muslim's act of piety – to give the child an Islamic education – conflicts with the state's policy to have children of all races and religions attending national schools. Second, we also posited that the state's refusal to expand the *madrasah* system and to allow Muslim girls to wear the *hijab* (veil) in national schools will cause frustration and conflict.

Education in Singapore

In contemporary Singapore, there is the Compulsory Education Act, which demands that all children who are citizens must enrol in a school that is part of the national education system, especially at the primary and secondary school levels. Within the system, there are 173 primary schools and 156 secondary schools, along with 18 post-secondary and pre-university schools, as well as several other special needs schools (Singapore Ministry of Education, 2006: 57). In 2006, there were 532,225 students enrolled in the national education system, accounting for over 95 per cent of all Singaporean children (Singapore Ministry of Education, 2006: 3). This highly centralized system, which has been described as being overtly techno-cratic, is designed to serve national interests, rather than any liberal or humanist purpose (see Pereira, 2008). The national interests are clearly to drive the economy, and to foster multiracialism. First, with regards to the economy, education is specif-ically designed to prepare Singaporeans to work in a globalized economy (see Gopinathan, 1996). The curriculum leans heavily towards scientific and technical education, with a considerable emphasis given to mathematics, science and also to instruction in the English language, especially in primary school. The logic behind this orientation was entirely the result of Singapore's separation from Malaysia in 1965. Because the country had no natural resources, Singapore had to survive by becoming a manufacturing hub for multinational corporations that were seeking cheap, disciplined and qualified labour (Gopinathan, 1996). This aspect of the educational policy has been successful, insofar as Singapore's economy rapidly industrialized, and there was sustained economic growth since 1965.

Second, the national education system was also designed to foster 'multiracialism' (Benjamin, 1976; Hill and Lian, 1995). Unlike other multicultural policies across the world, Singapore's multiracialism did not allow for parallel institutions because the state believed that education was also for the purposes of eliminating racial or ethnic conflict in society and to promote 'racial harmony'. In other words, schools were to function as a location for racial integration. Soon after independence, the Singapore government closed down vernacular schools – Chinese, Malay and Tamil stream schools – believing that these would foster 'mono-racialism', which was detrimental to national integration. Instead, the state created the national education system where every school would be multiracial in composition. Indeed, the state was so deter-mined to ensure the correct multiracial mix that it insisted that the racial composition in primary schools would have to be in line with the national racial composition of 75 per cent Chinese, 15 per cent Malay, and 10 per cent Indians and others (Gopinathan, 1996). In addition to having multiracial schools, the state wanted to ensure 'cultural preservation'. Thus, it implemented the mother-tongue policy, where the ethnic languages of each community is supported and encouraged by the state. Thus, in addition to all students learning the English language, and mathematics and science (which are taught in the English language), Chinese students must learn Mandarin, while Malay and Indian students must learn Malay and Tamil respectively. In this sense, the state wanted to overtly demonstrate that ethnic differences could be recognized (through cultural preservation) through a single broker institution rather than through separate parallel institutions (see Chua, 2004).

In this manner, the national educational system is able to serve the state's economic as well as social agenda simultaneously. While these principles are implemented for nearly all schools in the national educational system, the state has made two exceptions. The first exception is for the schools in the 'Special Assistance Plan' (SAP), and the second is for the Islamic Religious Schools, or the *madrasahs*. The national SAP schools are designed to train 'bicultural' students, which in Singapore's terms refers to students who have excellent proficiency in English and Mandarin language. In addition, students in the national SAP schools also take additional subjects such as Chinese history, Chinese literature and even Chinese music. Not surprisingly, almost the entire enrolment of the 13 national SAP schools consists of ethnic Chinese students. The Singapore government argues that the mono-racial composition of national SAP schools is unfortunate but necessary in order to train the next generation of Singaporean Chinese journalists, teachers and business persons. There are other 'mono-racial' schools, but these are mostly private educational institutions – such as the American School, the French School and the Indian School – that serve various expatriate communities. These do not come under the jurisdiction of the Ministry of Education, and Singapore citizens are not allowed to enrol in these. Hence, these are excluded from the discussion.

Singapore's *madrasahs*

In Singapore, *madrasahs* are schools devoted to Islamic studies and they have been in Singapore since British colonial times. Most of them began as part of a mosque, offering religious education to children (Chee, 2006). The first non-mosque *madrasah* – the *Madrasah* Alsagoff Al-Arabiyah – was established in Singapore in 1912. By 2007, there were six full-time *madrasahs* along with 27 part-time mosque *madrasahs*. The full-time *madrasahs* offer primary, secondary and pre-university level education. Some *madrasah* students will go on to further their studies in the local polytechnics and universities after their 'O' and 'A' level examinations respectively. At a *madrasah*, students not only take the basic quartet of subjects (English, Mathematics, Science and the Malay language), they have about six other subjects, which concern Islamic studies, some of which are taught in Arabic. Under sections 87 and 88 of the AMLA, the management of *madrasahs* is vested in MUIS. As mentioned earlier, full-time *madrasahs* serve the purpose of training Islamic specialists, scholars, teachers and administrators, which the country needs, for example to administer the *Syariah* (Islamic Law) Courts. According to the former Prime Minister Goh Chok Tong, *madrasahs* are of 'critical' importance because 'the future of the institution of Islam must be protected; Singapore needs Islamic teachers and these teachers should not have to go abroad for their education' (*Singapore Straits Times*, 2 May 2000).

However, the state limits the total number of places at the six full-time *madrasahs*, to around 4000 students in total (http://www.muis.gov.sg/cms/services/Madrasahs.aspx?id=1730). Considering that there are over 500,000 students in Singapore's national education system, the total enrolment of students in the *madrasah* system is less than 1 per cent. However, given that there are around 75,000 Malay-Muslim students (on the basis that they form 15 per cent of the total student population), then there clearly are insufficient places at the *madrasah* for them. The state insists that *madrasahs* are not meant to be an alternative educational option for Muslims. The state, being a typical interventionist technocracy, is worried about a potential over-supply of religious teachers, just as the state is also concerned about an over-supply of lawyers and medical doctors. Instead, the state wants 'ordinary' Malay-Muslim children to enrol in national schools in order to be economically prepared for work and to 'experience' multiracial integration. In May 2000, the *Singapore Straits Times* reported the views of the then-Prime Minister Goh Chok Tong on *madrasahs* in the article entitled 'Issue is future of Muslim children':

> 'The issue is the future of a younger generation of Muslim children,' he [then Prime Minister Goh Chok Tong] told reporters after the May Day Rally in the NTUC Lifestyle World Downtown East resort in Pasir Ris.
>
> He said: 'Do you want them to grow up all being religious teachers and religious preachers, or do you want them to be trained in IT, to be engineers, doctors, architects, professionals?'
>
> If the *madrasahs* were training 100 or 200 students a year, he said, 'I think we can live with that'.
>
> 'But if you are training 400, 500, 1,000, 2,000 in full-time *madrasahs* or in full-time religious education supplemented by some secular subjects, what will be the future of the Malay community?' he asked.
>
> (*Singapore Straits Times*, 2 May 2000)

We posited that there was a dilemma for pious Muslims in Singapore. On the one hand, the strong demand for places in the *madrasah* system is owing to the high level of religiosity within the community. On the other hand, the state is tightly controlling the enrolment in *madrasahs*. It is therefore highly likely that many parents had no choice but to enrol their children in national schools only after they were unable to get their children into a *madrasah*. We sought to understand the reason behind this strong demand for places in *madrasahs* in Singapore. Was it the case that many Muslim parents really want their children to be Islamic scholars and administrators? To understand this issue, as part of the Social Distance Project, we interviewed the respondents, asking for their views on *madrasah* education.

Valuing religious education

In general, of the respondents who described themselves as being 'devout' Muslims, about half of them indicated that they would prefer their children to enrol in a *madrasah* over national (secular) schools, especially after the improvements made to the *madrasah* system in 2000. However, only two have actually been able to enrol their children in *madrasahs*; for the rest who had children, their children were enrolled in national schools. Even of those that were currently unmarried or did not have children, many had a generally positive view towards the contemporary *madrasah* system. The three main reasons given were that they valued religious education, valued being in a religious environment and were disillusioned with the national school system.

When asked why they favoured *madrasahs* so much, all respondents indicated that 'religious education' was very important. Many said that learning to be 'good Muslims' was as important, if not more important, than secular pursuits.

> If any of the children do well enough [in a *madrasah*] to become an Islamic scholar, or teacher, then it would be wonderful. But even if they cannot, then the religious education that they received is worth a lot. They will be better Muslims.
>
> (Manager, male, 45)

> They will get success both in this life and the life thereafter. The knowledge taught in the *madrasah* is wider. The *madrasahs* inculcate in the children moral virtues. Plus, I have faith in the [quality of the] *madrasah* today. So many *madrasah* students have made it to the universities, not just the Islamic universities.
>
> (Housewife, 55)

Several other respondents also said that the *madrasah*'s longer educational period – it takes at least an extra year to complete primary and secondary education at the majority of *madrasahs* as compared to an average of ten years for the 'express stream' in national schools – was not a consideration. Some respondents believe that, while participating actively in the modernization of the country, they should not neglect their obligation of equipping their children with the necessary tools to cope in an age that is increasingly characterized by a crisis of modernity manifesting itself in moral decadence and purely materialist pursuits.

> Conviction and the belief in the need to impart the Islamic moral code led me to the conclusion that my child should be in the *madrasah*. I think that religious education will be an asset for a society that is entering into a post-industrial stage. Now I am not saying this to sound complex; Singapore has reached to the penultimate stage of its achievement. Similar to the West, we are witnessing a breakdown in the belief that the pursuit for material success should be the sole aim of life.
>
> (Teacher, male, 30s)

Perhaps the most interesting views on the issue of *madrasah* education came from the remaining half of the respondents that did not prefer to enrol their children in *madrasahs*. Ironically, they were in principle in favour of a *madrasah* education, but they were not convinced that Singapore's *madrasahs* could adequately provide this type of education. The main reason cited was the generally poor academic performance of *madrasah* students in national examinations. Some from this group of respondents said that they would be sending their children to a full-time *madrasah* but for what they saw as the inadequacies of the current *madrasah* system in Singapore.

> I am – in principle – in favour of sending children to a *madrasah*. However, from my own experience, the *madrasahs* here [in Singapore] do not provide top-class religious education, and also do not provide top-class academic education [referring to mathematics, science and the English language]. They are badly under-funded, and a lot of students who are there are problem kids, those who are naughty and misbehave. So these parents send these problem kids to *madrasahs* as if the *madrasah* is a reform school. This is not good for children who want to be properly trained in Islamic teachings. If the *madrasahs* got their act together, I would definitely send my children there.
>
> (Manager, male, 45)

> Today, many of the teachers in the *madrasahs* are informally trained, or only trained at the *madrasahs* itself. I believe very few have been to the good Islamic universities abroad; maybe only the principal. The standards there are so low. I hear things are getting better. The government is doing something about the educational standards, both in religious subjects and in academic subjects. Perhaps in the future, the *madrasah* will be much better. But generally, yes, I do believe if a child went to a good *madrasah,* he or she will be in a better position to be a good Muslim.
>
> (Engineer, male aged 30)

> Come to think of it, I should have sent my sons to the *madrasahs*. But during my sons' time, the 'drop-outs' went to *madrasahs*. Now, the *madrasahs'* standard has gone up. *Madrasahs* now can better balance the secular and religious subjects. My sons are going to be the heads of their families. It's good for them to have this balance. But back then, no. Of course, it would be taxing. But children have the capacity to learn. I wouldn't pressure them to be first, second or third [place] in class. I know by the time they are in upper primary they have to do 14 subjects and at secondary schools, they have to do 17 subjects.
>
> (Businesswoman, Female, 40s)

For the respondents that preferred their children to be enrolled in national schools, they indicated that learning about Islam was still very important. It was noticeable that this group of respondents said that their children were attending part-time religious classes, such as those being offered at the mosques in the evenings and weekends in lieu of being enrolled in a full-time *madrasah.*

> I think it is absolutely important that we must bring up our children to be good Muslims, and giving them this [religious] education is part of our duties.

Therefore, it is not an inconvenience to us that we have to send them to the classes after work at night or during weekends. It is a good thing.

(Financial Analyst, male, 40)

It is evident from the comments that the respondents do not just make their choices simply on emotive grounds. The process of instrumental rationalization plays an important role in their deliberation over whether to send their children to the full-time *madrasah*. To recapitulate, nearly all the respondents valued religious education. This finding is not surprising, because they are all self-described 'deeply religious' individuals. Their own ideal would be that their children could be enrolled in a *madrasah* that could satisfy both academic as well as religious needs, as many were pragmatic enough to know that should their children not qualify for higher religious education (in Islamic universities, for example), then they would still be able to survive in Singapore.

A religious environment

Another view that emerged from the interviews was that most respondents felt that the *madrasah* provided a proper 'Islamic environment' for their children. This view seemed to be very important for the respondents and they indicated that the Islamic environment allowed their children to be free from a secular public/private sphere dichotomous worldview. In other words, the respondents felt that the *madrasah*'s environment enabled their children to practise religion without any inhibitions.

> *Madrasahs* are good because they create an Islamic environment for the children. This means they do not need to worry about meals, or whatever. Also, the classrooms separate the boys from the girls. I think this is good.
>
> (Civil servant, male, 36)
>
> I have to constantly remind my children to be extra careful about food and drink when they go to [a national] school. They shouldn't share utensils, and must take care at the canteen. If this was a *madrasah,* we don't need to worry about these things.
>
> (Civil servant, male, 50)

The implication is that neither of these considerations – which are evidently very important to these individuals – is met at a national school. Also, this position is not surprising because many pious Muslims have a high level of *halal* consciousness (as discussed in the previous chapter).

This research also found that several Muslim parents would prefer to send their children to *madrasahs* because of their concern for the Muslim dress code, especially for their daughters. Many cited the teaching that Muslim females must be modestly dressed at all times in public. For many of them, modesty involves wearing the *tudung,* which is the Malay word for the Islamic headscarf. In Singapore, the term *tudung* is a shorthand for the *hijab*, which is the Islamic dress code that involves the covering of the arms and the legs, along with all other parts of the body, as will be discussed in the next chapter. However, on the issue of school uniforms, some respondents lamented that they did not feel comfortable that their daughters who were in national schools were 'forced' to wear uniforms that 'did not conform to Islamic teachings'.

> I think that the Singapore government does not understand Islam very well. Do they not know that their refusal to allow true believers to follow Islamic teaching is very upsetting? You see, the *tudung,* just like being a good Muslim, is a choice. Once you make that choice, you have to live like that. So wearing the *tudung* means the person is living like a good Muslim. How can the state ask us not to be a good Muslim?
>
> (Civil servant, male, 50)

> Actually, the problem goes beyond just the *tudung*. The whole uniform is not appropriate, especially for girls. And the PE (physical education) attire is even worse, just a t-shirt and shorts; this is not acceptable for good Muslims. What I don't understand is why can't they allow the girls to wear long-sleeve t-shirts and track pants?
>
> (Administrator, male, 45)

The issue of school uniforms among devout Muslims has recently become a highly fractious affair in Singapore. In general, the Singapore state does not allow any variation to the set uniforms in national schools and as a result wearing the *tudung* is disallowed. In many ways, the Singapore government's argument is exactly the same as the position of governments in the UK and France on the *hijab* or Islamic veil in their respective school systems, where religious exceptions are seen as a threat to its multicultural ideology (see Bowen, 2007). However, in Singapore the Ministry of Education does make exceptions if the religion prescribes (by way of religious laws) the wearing of certain clothes. For example, since it is prescribed by their religion, Sikh males do not cut any facial or head hair after the onset of puberty. The state allows them to wear turbans and to keep beards in school. However, the state has made clear that the wearing of the crucifix or the *tudung* is not allowed, because these are not considered to be mandatory religious objects. This position is clearly contradictory because according to guidelines issued by MUIS, females should wear the *hijab* when they reach puberty, as we will discuss in the next chapter.

The contradictions in the state's uniform policy caused conflict between the Muslim community and the state. As early as 1999, a female student from Tanjong Katong Secondary School was suspended from school for her wearing of the *tudung* (*Singapore Straits Times,* 9 June 2002). Interestingly, this episode was not reported at the time and only surfaced after the *tudung* incidents of 2002. This student eventually quit the national education system to study privately. This incident was perhaps the first sign that devout Muslims were keen to assert their religious choice to the state. In October 2001, a petition signed by over 3300 Singaporeans of various social backgrounds was submitted to Prime Minister Goh Chok Tong, Abdullah Tarmugi (the then Minister in Charge of Muslim Affairs) and the local media (http://www.thinkcentre.org/article.cfm?ArticleID=1367, 'Petition for *Aurat* in National Schools', October 2001). The state remained silent regarding this petition.

This was followed by the main '*tudung* issue' which began in early 2002, when four Muslim parents insisted that their seven-year-old children be allowed to attend schools in the national education system but wear the *tudung* over and above the uniform. Interestingly some of the parents who were interviewed by the local media claimed that they were ardent 'believers' in the national educational system whose facilities and infrastructure, they claimed, were far superior to that of the *madrasahs* (*Singapore Straits Times*, 1 February 2002). The only 'setback' of national schools was the ban on the Islamic dress code. The schools responded by barring the students from entering the compounds, and suspending the students until they returned in normal school uniform. In the subsequent two years, the whole *tudung* issue was politicized and became a very controversial topic that affected state–Muslim relations (see Suzaina, 2005). Although this chapter does not seek to revisit or even explain the '*tudung* issue', the case is relevant because many devout Muslim parents felt that the national guidelines for uniforms were not in accordance with Islamic principles. As a result many were sending their daughters to the *madrasahs* to ensure that the modest Islamic dress code was observed (Dayang, 2003: 14, 64). Interestingly, the *Mufti* – Singapore's highest ranking religious cleric – made a comment about the *tudung* versus uniforms issue when he said 'The no-*tudung* rule lasts only for a few hours when the pupils are in school. Education is more important' (*Singapore Straits Times*, 6 February 2002). We posited that the *Mufti* chose to downplay the situation, even though there is an official MUIS guideline that states that females have to wear the *hijab* after puberty. However, the overall frustration and anger from within the Malay-Muslim community over the *tudung* issue showed that there was a segment of pious Muslims in Singapore who were not particularly convinced of the *Mufti*'s position on the *tudung* in national schools.

In our research, some respondents felt that the government's policies were too severe and rigid.

> But this is a silly notion; I honestly don't think a Singaporean worries about this, other than the government. The Chinese don't bother about this, the Christians are also not going to bother … why does the state think that allowing the *tudung* will lead to a slippery slope where everybody will make their own demands? There should be a live and let live mentality, not a one size fits all!
>
> (Accountant, male, 40)

Overall it is evident that devout Muslim parents view the *madrasah's* environment as being better at allowing their children to become good Muslims, when compared to the national schools. Although we did not directly gather any views that pious Muslims would prefer to enrol their children, especially daughters, in *madrasahs* in order to avoid the secular public school environment, the very high value placed by our respondents on the Islamic environment might suggest that there is a high level of unhappiness with the public school environment.

Disillusionment with national schools

Another strong view held by many respondents was their sense of disillusionment with the national educational curriculum. Most felt that, while academic education was acceptable at national schools, they were not making life any easier for Muslims. Several brought up the uniform and issue of the Islamic dress code again, but there were some who pointed to other concerns. The first concern is that the national school system tended to focus only on academic performance and 'nothing else'. Even though there were segments within the curriculum that were designed to build moral character of the students – this included the Civics and Moral Education Programme at the primary school level – to most parents in our study, these were totally insufficient. Previously, the state even had introduced the Religious Knowledge curriculum, which was made compulsory in secondary schools in 1984. Islamic, Buddhist, Confucian, Bible, Hindu and Sikh studies were introduced. However, the government in October 1989 announced that they were scrapping this curriculum amidst fears that the programme had resulted in the opposite effect of actually emphasizing the differences between religions. It was then replaced by a Civics and Moral Education Programme. However, the problem was not only that the Civics and Moral Education Programme was relegated to one 30-minute lesson per week, it was also that the core academic subjects were seen as being 'all important'.

> I feel so sorry for some of the children that go into Singapore's schools. So much pressure on exams; the teachers are always pressuring the students to work so hard. Even stay back after school to do more work. They are children, let them be. Let them perform to whatever they perform. Why push them so hard? Is doing well the only thing in life? I don't accept this, but if we don't cooperate to push our children in these schools, then they will fall to the back of class, and everyone will make fun of them, or get marginalized by the teachers. So terrible.
>
> (Engineer, male, 40)

> Education should not just be about scoring 'A's' in exams every time. Education must be about bringing up children to be good people in the end. I understand that they must have the basics to find work later in life, but schools don't do anything to improve the student's character, or morality. I believe that at a *madrasah*, the total development of the child is taken care of. Isn't that how it should be?
>
> (Manager, male, 36)

The views of these Muslim parents do not seem out of tandem with some Singaporeans who have chosen to migrate to other countries, citing the uncompromising education system as among one of the main reasons which led to their eventual departure. In addition, most of Singapore's migrants have attained a relatively good educational level and belong to the more privileged class, judging by average annual income. Cheung (1991) brings to our attention that about 40,000 Singaporeans emigrated in the years 1986 to 1990. Hui (1992) is of the opinion that the loss of human capital investment is potentially huge because about 90 per cent of them had at the very least secondary education and 45 per cent were working in the technical, professional or managerial sectors. While some migrated because they sought better working conditions and remuneration, many claimed they did not want their children to be put through the rigid grind of Singapore's highly stressful education system.

Among other reasons given by those who migrated from Singapore are the perceived difficulty in acquiring material assets for example cars and landed property, the lifestyle in Singapore as being too hectic and stressful (no less because of a demanding education system) and the existence of an omnipresent government (Sullivan and Gunasekaran, 1994; Yap, 1991). This has led to former Prime Minister Goh Chok Tong making a distinction between the 'stayers' and the 'quitters'. 'Stayers' is a term that refers to Singaporeans who do not leave merely for the lure of 'greener pastures' abroad and instead display a commitment by choosing to stay put. 'Quitters', as one might have guessed, is a reference to those who give up on Singapore and what it stands for. And what most people think the country stands for is economic growth, and more economic growth only. As such, citizens are not valued for being themselves, but are seen by the state as nothing more than 'human resources'. This meant that every person needed to be 'economically useful'. Two respondents, who were civil servants did not want to criticize the national educational system; however, their views on this issue were telling.

> In Singapore, the reality is that we must be economically useful in the future. There is after all no welfare system here. In this sense, Singapore is a materialistic and cruel world. Unemployed means you will starve to death, and nobody will help you. So as a parent, I am duty bound to provide for my children's future. That is why I prefer them to go to national schools now. Morality – we can take care of that by sending the children to mosque classes, and we as parents must set the right examples.
>
> (Civil servant, male, 50)

> The [national] school system gives our children good values such as hard work, and perseverance. And the family and the [Malay-Muslim] community must then play its part to give the children the other values that are important, religiosity and morality.
>
> (Civil servant, male, 42)

Another source of unhappiness among many of the respondents related to the state's claim that national schools are better for promoting racial harmony, or improving inter-racial or inter-religious tolerance. Most respondents indicated that the state's claim is only 'all talk and no action'. They do not take for granted that sending their children to national schools is a sufficient precursor to inter-religious understanding.

How are schools actually supposed to foster better inter-racial relations? I think the government's idea is that just throw all the kids together, and everything will be all right. But the school doesn't do anything to promote tolerance or understanding.

(Administrator, male, 36)

You know, I think the [national] school system actually undoes racial harmony. I mean, kids are kids, and they play with each other at the playground downstairs, and don't think about race or religion. Then when they go to school, they are told that they are different – different race, different religion. And that's when the problems start. I don't think that the [national] school system does what it claims.

(Manager, male, 40)

One respondent suggested that being in a (mono-racial) *madrasah* need not necessarily be detrimental for race relations:

Why does the state think that just because the *madrasah* is made up of all Malays that it will be a problem? I mean, when these children come home, they have people of all races living next door! So what is the problem? I don't see any problem.

(Accountant, male, aged 40)

This is an allusion to the government's policy of imposing ethnic quotas on public housing where about 90 per cent of Singaporeans live. We thus have seen the elimination of particular communities living in ethnic enclaves for example Chinatown (for Chinese), Geylang Serai (for Malays) and Serangoon (for Indians). The state has done its best to disperse the various communities into various residential areas to do away with the colonial legacy of ethnic enclaves. Ironically, since the state housing policy is already successful, Muslim parents do not see the need for schools to also be an avenue for social integration.

State management of the *madrasahs*

In October 2007, in a bid to 'upgrade' the *madrasah* system, the Singapore government made a dramatic policy shift. Concerned about educational standards, the state introduced the 'Joint *Madrasah* System (JMS)'. Significantly, only three of the six full-time *madrasahs*, however, committed themselves. Under this scheme, beginning 2009, both the *Madrasahs* Aljunied and Al-Arabiah will cease enrolling primary pupils and focus on secondary education whereas the Al-Irsyad *madrasah* will specialize specifically in primary education and function as a feeder school to the other two *madrasahs*. Al-Arabiah will be focusing more on the 'academic subjects' while Aljunied will be leaning towards 'religious subjects' (*Berita Harian*, 29 October 2007). MUIS will aid these three *madrasahs* to raise funds. Amongst the purported benefits is a salary raise amongst the *madrasah* teachers. The revision in salary is important according to the MUIS President: 'We will do a thorough study to try and improve pay. We have to compete for teachers so the pay must be attractive. With these steps, we can ensure our kids have the best teachers' (*Singapore Straits Times*, 27 October, 2007; 30 October 2007). *Madrasah* teachers will also undergo further training and experienced teachers will be recruited from national schools. Interestingly, both the all-female *madrasahs*, Alsagoff and Al-Maarif, chose not to participate in this endeavour.

The state has given the following reasons for the implementation of this new strategy: the move will raise the academic standards and make the *madrasahs* more efficient. The chairman of *Madrasah* Aljunied, *Ustaz* Pasuni Maulan, foresees this move as easing the pressure on his Islamic religious school, 'We won't be burdened with preparations for PSLE, although our teachers are doing their best to prepare students for it these few years ... We can focus on educating students, and not worry about getting teachers and parents to help raise funds' (*Singapore Straits Times*, 27 October 2007). Dr Yaacob, the Minister in Charge of Muslim Affairs, hoped that the remaining three *madrasahs* would join the JMS later, and called the effort a 'bold and progressive step'. He gave assurances that MUIS would extend support in preparing the students to meet the Primary School Leaving Examination (PSLE) standard and also support the three *madrasahs* with funds, teachers, administrative systems and management teams. Dr Yaacob said if the Malay-Muslim community wanted to benefit from Singapore's world-class education system, it must continue to adopt 'an open, positive attitude towards learning and education' (*Singapore Straits Times*, 27 October 2007).

While actual details about the new JMS system remain unclear, it is evident to us that the overall number of places at the *madrasahs* will decline. Given that there is already a very strong demand for places at *madrasahs,* the limiting of 400 places will come as a serious concern to devout Muslim parents who not only want their children to be groomed as religious scholars but those who want their daughters especially to be in a schooling environment where the dress code is in accordance to Islamic principles, and by implication, where the environment is unlike the national education system.

Our research has found that pious Muslim parents valued the *madrasahs* for promoting religiosity (through an Islamic education), and providing a proper Muslim environment for their children. However, due to the technocratic strategies of the state, and the increasing religiosity of Muslims, there simply would not be enough places at Singapore's *madrasahs* to meet the demand. The state is not only worried about an over-supply of Islamic scholars and administrators, but also fears enclavement. It insists that 'ordinary' or 'regular' Malay-Muslim children attend national schools so that they can integrate with the other races and religions. Yet, by ignoring Muslim religiosity, the state is creating a problematic situation. The crux of the problem is the issue of proper Islamic dress code, which appears to be at odds with the state's uniform policy. Malay-Muslims view the banning of the *tudung* as being contradictory, especially since the state allows some other religions to alter the uniform (for example, the turban is allowed for Sikhs), and also since MUIS – a statutory board – has stated clearly that wearing the *hijab* is mandatory for all females after the onset of puberty. Still, the state refuses to relent.

That the state also refuses to expand the *madrasah* system to meet the increasing demand is also viewed as problematic by the Malay-Muslim community. If the state is so worried about enclavement, then why does the state allow for other types of 'mono-racial' schools? For example, the bicultural SAP schools are almost exclusively all-Chinese in composition. These contradictions will ultimately lead to some in the Malay-Muslim community feeling that they are being negatively discriminated against and socially marginalized, which would in turn lead to some degree of alienation from the society. Already, many are using the *madrasah* as a comfort zone whereby they can practise their religion freely. *Madrasahs* are viewed as having an environment where Muslims believe that their children can become 'good Muslims', as opposed to the national school environment where they are denied some religious rights (such as wearing the *hijab* for female students after the onset of puberty). As such, many ended up enrolling their children in national schools grudgingly and unhappily, simply because there are either not enough places in the current six full-time *madrasah* schools or they did not believe that the *madrasah* system is ready to provide their children with a sound education in the 'secular' subjects.

We thus posit that the real leakage rate from national schools by pious Muslims would be much higher if there were appropriate options. Following on from that, the degree of social distancing would therefore be very high, as pious Muslims – if they had the opportunity – would seek to exit the national school system in favour of the safe zone of the *madrasah*. This might in turn imply that religiosity would automatically lead pious individuals to distance themselves from the 'impure' out of religious self-preservation. Yet, while religiosity is applicable to the Singapore case, it is not necessarily the key factor. There is some attempt at distancing themselves to preserve religious purity, but we also argue that the state's inconsistent and contradictory policy contributes to the problem. If the state could accommodate the religious obligations of the Muslims, as it currently does for some other religions, then we predict that many pious Muslim parents would not feel the need to send their children (especially daughters) to the *madrasah*. For example, we do not foresee that *hijab* wearing female students would pose any greater threat to Singapore's multiracial integration than Sikh boys wearing a turban. In sum, we feel that if the state allowed the *hijab* and was more careful about *halal* consciousness, many pious Muslims would be less inclined to exit the national school system. This would therefore mean that more Muslim children would experience multiracial integration.

This has a further knock-on effect at the *madrasahs* itself. Our view is that currently, by using the *madrasah* mainly as a safe zone, many pious Muslim parents are taking up places from those who are genuinely interested in or intent on becoming Islamic scholars and administrators. This might probably mean that the resources at each of the *madrasahs* need not be so severely stretched as they currently are due to the heavy intake of students, in turn probably leading to a better Islamic education all round.

Is accommodation so impossible?

> Faith is important to human beings, and a positive force for society. But greater religious fervour also means more activities within the same religious group, and inevitably less interaction between different groups. This can weaken our social cohesion as a nation, unless we actively work to bring the different groups together. We need to foster more interaction between the different races and religions. We cannot force this, but we must do our best to encourage it. Singaporeans need to know one another, socialise together, and make friends who belong to different races and religions. We must also preserve public spaces like our schools, workplaces and community areas, as shared places where everyone belongs and feels comfortable. This is the way for Singaporeans to understand one another, widen the common ground which we all share together, and so strengthen racial and religious harmony.
>
>   Prime Minister Lee Hsien Loong, in a speech given at the official opening of The Harmony Centre at An-Nahdah Mosque, 7 October 2006.
>
>   http://www.pap.org.sg/articleview.php?id=1252&mode=&cid=23

Based on the views expressed in the Social Distance Project, it is possible to extrapolate the view of the larger Muslim community on the *madrasahs*. There are those who 'believe in the *madrasah* system'. These are parents who would like their children to be Islamic scholars, but some also wished to see that their children would become good Muslims through gaining a foundation in Islamic studies. Furthermore, they argued that since all *madrasahs* in Singapore also teach academic subjects, their children's economic future would not be jeopardized. In other words, even if their children do not become Islamic clerics, administrators or scholars, they will be able to find 'regular' jobs. Hence, for them, *madrasahs* offer the best combination of religious and secular education. Viewed objectively, it is precisely for this group that the *madrasahs* in Singapore exist.

However, we believe there are also some who have turned to the *madrasahs* only because they are disillusioned with the national school system. Some perceive that the national education system is merely preparing their children for materialist pursuits. They feel that the *madrasahs* provide a better alternative in inculcating the right moral values in their children. Another complaint is that the national school system does not allow their children to be 'good Muslims', for example, female students are not allowed to wear the *tudung* to national schools. As such, some have turned to the *madrasahs* as a means to accommodate this religiosity. In many ways, given that the number of places in the *madrasah* system is very limited, it could be argued that this situation is not healthy, as some of these students might be taking places away from those who are genuinely serious about gaining an Islamic education.

For the first group, those that believe in the *madrasah* system, they are not really practising social distancing, which refers to the practice of excluding themselves from secular or multicultural life in order to protect their religiosity. Instead, they are simply exercising a choice to train their children to be religious scholars. It is the other group, who are disillusioned with the national educational system, that might appear to be practising social distancing, as they turned to the *madrasah* in order to maintain religious 'purity' but were not necessarily against secular education or particularly keen on their children becoming Islamic scholars. Based on the second group, our data suggests that the social distancing was not 'spontaneous' but perhaps externally induced by, ironically, state policy. As several respondents have reported, those within this group would actually prefer to send their children to national schools but are 'prevented' by state policies, such as the no-*tudung* rule.

Singapore's system of multiculturalism is a delicate but sometimes contradictory balancing act. On the one hand, it purports to allow cultural and religious autonomy; on the other, it insists on multicultural interaction and mixing, especially in public institutions. Since the state feels that it cannot be seen to show favour to any one group, it has therefore rejected the possibility of allowing some variation to the school uniforms in national schools; however, this lack of flexibility has 'pushed' some students away from the national schools to the *madrasahs*. From a policy perspective, it is worth rethinking whether the Singapore state's rigid stand on this issue is doing more harm than good, especially since it does believe that mixed schools are generally better for social integration. Also, given that the state constantly uses a 'cost-benefit' analysis, it is worth asking whether this rigid stand on uniforms, for example, is causing an unnecessary added load on the *madrasahs,* which might ultimately affect the state's own objectives of training high quality Islamic scholars. Still, this chapter was not written as a policy review; instead, its aim was to better understand the concept of enclavement and social distancing.

6 The body and piety

The *hijab* and marriage

Introduction

In our quest to understand if practising acts of piety would lead to social distancing, we have finally arrived at the body itself. To recapitulate, our interest has been in how religiosity might lead individuals to physically and socially create social distance between themselves and the religiously impure. In the previous chapters on dining and education, we have shown how pious Muslims managed their religiosity within a secular society by performing various forms and degrees of social distancing. For dining, we saw pious Muslims practising defensive forms of distancing in order to continue participating in public life while maintaining their religiosity. However, on education and educational issues, because of concerns about the lack of religiosity in public schools, some have chosen to place their children within the safe comfort of the *madrasahs*.

In this chapter, we wanted to understand how pious Muslims, especially women, in practising acts of piety, distanced their own bodies from the impure. More specifically, we focused on two aspects: veiling and interpersonal relationships. As part of the Social Distance Project, we asked respondents how they felt about maintaining physical purity, and if this caused any conflicts in public life which was both secular and multicultural. The first aspect, veiling, refers to the Islamic rules and teachings on 'modest' dressing for women. Within Islam, the veil is known as wearing the *hijab* (modest clothes) to cover the *awrah* (Arabic) or *aurat* (Malay); these are parts of the body that are forbidden to be exposed (except to their husbands). We therefore sought to understand whether the religious requirement to wear the *hijab* would in any way lead to social conflict within public life in Singapore. The second act of piety centres on interpersonal relations; how far would pious Muslims, especially women, go when it comes to having relationships – including friendships or marriages – with non-Muslims? Would religion be a factor that influenced their choice of friends? Would they consider marrying people of other faiths, or would they only practise homogamy (marrying those of the same religion)? If religion indeed influenced Muslims to only interact (socially) with other Muslims, then this would be an indicator of social distance. In the discussion that follows, we included the respondent's marital status as this may affect their views towards veiling or inter-personal relations.

The *hijab*

As we saw in the previous chapter, it is clear that the *tudung* (headscarf) was a source of controversy in Singapore's national schools. Technically, the *tudung* is just one component of the *hijab*, which translated means 'modest' or 'proper' dress code. The *hijab* involves covering the *aurat*, which refers to parts of the body that are forbidden to be exposed. In the *Qur'an*, the logic of the *hijab* is explained in Chapter 24 (An-Nur, The Light) Verse 31.

> And say to the believing women that they should lower their gaze and guard their modesty; that they should not display their beauty and ornaments except what (must ordinarily) appear thereof; that they should draw their veils over their bosoms and not display their beauty except to their husbands, their fathers, their husband's fathers, their sons, their husbands' sons, their brothers or their brothers' sons, or their sisters' sons, or their women, or the slaves whom their right hands possess, or male servants free of physical needs, or small children who have no sense of the shame of sex; and that they should not strike their feet in order to draw attention to their hidden ornaments. And O ye Believers! Turn ye all together towards Allah, that ye may attain Bliss.
>
> (Translated by Abdullah Yusuf Ali, 1989)

In Singapore, MUIS has issued the following guidelines on the *hijab:*

> Why must a Muslimah wear the *Hijab*?
> Islam states that when a Muslimah has reached puberty, it is mandatory for her to observe the Islamic rules of modesty. This entails the following principles:
> The entire body has to be clothed, including the head and neck except for the face and palms of the hands. The clothes worn must be opaque and sufficiently thick so as not to reveal what is beneath and it must be loose, such that it does not define the contour of the body distinctly.
> This ruling is enjoined clearly in both the Islamic sources of Jurisprudence, the *Qur'an* and the *hadith* (Traditions of the Prophet). However, Islam does not specify the style of dressing, with regard to colour and design. It can be adapted to any style based on the prevailing culture and norms of the society as long as the above principles are maintained.
> The way Muslims dress is only one facet of modesty, Muslims have to manifest modesty in every aspect of their lives, including in behaviour, manners, speech and appearance.
> Is covering the face compulsory for Muslim women?
> The ulama differ in opinion on the covering of the face for women. The first opinion is that it is *wajib*. They based their opinion on verse 59, *surah* Al-Ahzab, in which they infer that lowering the garment in that verse implies covering the face too. The ulama in this group then differ among themselves on which part of the face must be covered and which part can be uncovered. Some of them are of the view that the whole face should be covered including the eyes. Some said only one eye can be visible. Some said both eyes can be

visible but not other parts of the face including the eyebrow. Some said the eye and forehead can be uncovered.

The second opinion is that covering the face is *mustahab* or even *wajib* if there is a *fitnah*.

The third opinion is that the face is not *aurat*, thus it is not necessary to cover the face. The ulama in this group then differ on the range of *aurat* for women. Some said that only the face and the hands below the wrist are not *aurat*. Some said the face and arm are not *aurat*. Some add to the list by saying that the feet is also not *aurat*.

The original position of Imam Syafii is that covering the face is *wajib*. But the accepted position of most ulama of the Syafii *Mazhab* is that the face and hands below the wrist are not *aurat*. A few ulama of the Syafii *mazhab* stated that the feet is also not *aurat* outside *solat*.

(http://www.muis.gov.sg/eservices/faqs/muis_faqmain.asp?strItemChoice =2005329125753&strSubItemChoice=2005329125811&action=SHOW-TOPICS&m_strTopicSysID=200732716628)

With regards to wearing of the *hijab* or the *tudung* in national schools and the resulting controversy of 2002, the issue was very basic. Some Muslims felt that wearing it was for religious obligations – to protect the female body from the impure. However, the state interpreted the act as a divisive element, because the pupils would not be in uniform (inclusive) but instead become socially exclusive. Extrapolating from this case, in this section we sought to ask whether the *hijab* was in fact a symbol of exclusion from the secular sphere or simply a defensive distancing for adult Muslim women. It needs to be pointed out that in contemporary, secular and multicultural Singapore, despite the guideline from MUIS, the *hijab* is not mandatory in the sense that non-conformity is not enforceable by any law, as it is in other societies such as Saudi Arabia where the *hijab* is mandatory. Thus, for adult Muslim women in Singapore, given that there are no formal legal sanctions against non-conformity, wearing or not wearing the headscarf becomes, in effect, a matter of choice.

Given the fact that a choice was available, why did Muslim women in fact choose to wear the *hijab*? Was it for obligatory religious reasons, or perhaps an act of self-conscious personal protection? If so, protection from whom? Or was this act undertaken to exclude oneself from the secular sphere? Would veiling lead to or have the unintended consequence of creating a pious enclave? To find out, we analysed data collected from the 20 middle-class Muslim women who were from within the Social Distance Project sample. While all 20 respondents described themselves as being 'religious' or 'very religious', only ten women were currently 'full-time' wearers of the *hijab* at the time of the research.

Wearing religiosity

First, we sought to understand the relationship(s) between wearing the *hijab* and religiosity. All the respondents, including those who did not wear the *hijab* all the time, were fully aware that the *hijab* is a mandatory religious obligation. It was interesting that when asked why they wore the *hijab*, most of the respondents gave a 'religious' or 'doctrinal' reason.

> Besides it is a dress code for Muslim ladies, when our God says in Surah An-Nur [*Qur'an*, Chapter 24] '… put on your headscarf and lower your gaze as a sign of modesty'. So from here, it also helps to minimize crimes, and fighting, when people stare at each other they will start to find problems. And it is practised by Muslims when the ladies reach puberty. They are told to put on this scarf whenever they meet men (who are) outsiders (i.e. not their *mahram*, family).
>
> (Full time private tutor, 22, single)

However, when they were then asked if they wore the *hijab* only because of a religious obligation, all the current wearers denied this. Instead, many said that 'understanding the meaning' was a very important reason for wearing the *hijab*.

> Yes, it is an obligation. But we must understand why it is an obligation. If we wear [the *hijab*] purely as obligation, then it defeats the purpose. When I wear, I know what it means: it means we must be modest and chaste. We must be pure. We must behave, and we are supposed to carry a message, and that is the message of being a woman that is chaste.
>
> (Social Worker, 27, single)

> I think it is not good if the Muslimah wore the *tudung* only because it is a religion obligation. We must understand what modesty means, and also to live our lives accordingly. No point wearing the *tudung* and do bad things, or do not live in accordance to the *Qur'an*.
>
> (Graduate Researcher, 23, single)

Following this, many respondents suggested that, not only was it necessary to understand the significance of the *hijab*, but one must also be 'ready'. More specifically, being ready here meant being ready to make a full-time commitment to being a good Muslim.

> As a Muslim, I believe it is an obligation. But then I also believe that one has to be ready, one has to be motivated by the right reasons to be wearing the scarf, whenever they go out, in the presence of those who are not their *mahram* [people of the opposite sex that they are not related to].
>
> (Human Resource Manager, 43, single)

Indeed, this feeling was even more pronounced among those who were currently not full-time wearers of the *hijab*. Many spoke of needing to feel 'ready' before making the commitment to wear the *hijab* full time.

> Once I am ready [to wear the *hijab* full time], I cannot change my mind. I have to be fully committed to all the values. So for example, after wearing, cannot go clubbing or hang out with men who are not related.
>
> (Fresh University Graduate, 23, single)

In a similar vein, another phrase that was commonly used by respondents was that the Muslimah must be 'sincere' when she wears the *hijab*.

> What's the point if you are the kind of person who wears the *hijab* and you start to yell and scream at people for no reason, or you don't behave well, or rather you are impolite? That's not being a good Muslim. So I think it is essential that values should come first.
>
> (Social worker, 27, single)

Another refrain that emerged from the interviews was the notion of 'choice'. Although Islam is fairly clear about the *hijab*, especially for women, nearly all of the respondents still indicated that 'the choice' to wear the *hijab* was important. When asked if they thought the *hijab* should be mandatory for Muslim women, nearly all the respondents disagreed with this view.

> I don't think this would be a good idea. But if it is mandatory, there will be a lot of people who won't like it. And there will be those who don't understand why they are wearing it. So if they have to wear it, they would just be hypocritical because they don't know. So for them it [the *tudung*] is just a piece of cloth.
>
> (Graduate student, 23, single)

Interestingly, although 'being religious' or being 'a Good Muslim' is the most common response as to why they wear the *hijab*, some argued that a woman can still be religious or a 'Good Muslim' even if she does not wear the *hijab*. For example, according to one respondent who does not wear the *hijab* even though her mother and several other family members do, the main issue is 'being good' rather than the *hijab* itself.

> In terms of whether it is necessary or not, if you want to base it on the *Qur'an*, there is actually no … there is actually no particular paragraph or verse that says that women must put on the headscarf. It's just that they say that women must, I think it is for *hijab*, they must cover their *aurat* but that is subject to whose interpretation it is. And most of the time the interpretation is they must be decently dressed but that is nothing to do with hair coverings but in the Prophet Muhammad's time his wives were taken as very clear examples of what a good Muslim woman should be, and they put on something I guess the outer covering and it would include their hair if I am not mistaken. So, for me, it [wearing] is not necessary. As long as I'm decent, what I think is decently dressed, that's enough.
>
> (Librarian, 36, single)

Many respondents spoke of 'being ready' to put on the *hijab*. All the respondents – except one who attended a *madrasah* in Singapore – did not wear the *hijab* on a 'full-time' basis until they left the national school system simply because the national school system does not allow for wearing the *tudung*. Within this group, some further reported that they were 'part-time' wearers during their school days. In other words, they put on the *hijab* when they were in public but took it off if they had to attend national school. Given these external circumstances, for some respondents, since they had some choice as to when they would finally wear the *hijab* 'full time', this act had become a very important rite of passage. This was the experience of one respondent.

> I remember that my parents encouraged me to wear the *tudung* full time after I left school. But I didn't, immediately. It was only in my 20s that I felt ready to wear the *tudung*. My then boyfriend, who is now my husband, said, 'Are you sure you're ready?' I said, 'Yes, I am ready.' I made a personal choice at what I felt was the right time, as I had felt I was finally ready. Ready to commit myself fully to Islam and the Islamic way of life.
>
> (Teacher, 31, married)

The same logic also seemed to apply to non-wearers, as well.

> I'm not prepared to wear the *tudung* today. Mentally, I'm not prepared. I mean like I said, you have to have a proper conduct, portray the right image, and I'm not ready yet to wear. Yes of course I will wear. When, I don't know yet. I don't think I should be telling myself by 35 or 40 I have to wear. I will wear when I feel I am ready. One day I might just wake up and my heart tell me you know, it's time … it is the right time and I will just do it [wear the *hijab*].
>
> (Customer Service Representative, 33, Married)

> The most important reason is actually believing the actual values of why you should be wearing it? So for me, I believe that I don't want to be forced, and I want to be sure that I am fully committed to it. So I don't want to be wearing it today and not tomorrow. But I don't want to wear it without the full intention of being permanent and being committed to it, because that would give them [family] even more sin to bear for myself.
>
> (Financial analyst, 22, single)

While the respondents were fully aware that wearing the *hijab* is a religious obligation, our study has shown that some intellectual reflection on the practice has also taken place. This is on the surface not surprising since the women interviewed were all 'middle class', highly educated and mostly employed in professional jobs. They therefore would be more likely to seek some reflexive understanding of the religious practice than the less educated, working-class women who were more likely to be ritualistic in their adherence to practice. Furthermore, Singapore's external secular environment, where there are generally no strict sanctions against not wearing the *hijab*, has allowed these women to embrace the idea of 'choice' as central to their manifestation of religiosity. In other words, these women choose to be pious rather than being pressured into piety. Thus, for these women, the wearing of the *hijab* had become a rite of passage, which marked an exit from a secular life into being aware about leading a fully committed religious life. This suggested that the binary view that *hijab* wearers were religious and non-wearers were irreligious was almost certainly false. Indeed, those who were interviewed for this study who were not full-time wearers were not being hypocritical when they identified themselves as being 'religious'. In fact, for the current non-wearers, since all of them indicated that they will wear the *hijab* full time later in life, they seem to be working towards and looking forward to that important day. As such, the act of wearing the *hijab* has come to mean much more than if they were simply socialized or pressured into the act out of mere custom.

Distancing?

> The veil [*hijab*] serves as a highly visible symbol of Muslim identity around the world.
>
> (Brenner, 1996: 693)

We also sought to understand if pious Muslim women used the *hijab* to distance themselves or to protect their bodies from the impure. The impure might include certain environments or places, or it might also include people who are perceived to be religiously impure in the sense that they do not live in accordance with religious practices. To examine this, we first investigated whether full-time *hijab* wearers tended to keep their distance from non-wearers. In this regard, our data on the *hijab* suggested that most of the wearers reported that the majority of their close female Muslim friends were also wearers. The question was whether their preference for the fellowship of similar *hijab* wearers was in fact an attempt to remain spiritually pure by avoiding the non-wearers, who might be perceived to be less pure in religious terms. For example, the critical aspect of the *hijab* was the covering up of the *aurat*; hence, exposure was technically 'sinful'. Thus, it could be suggested that those pious Muslim women would prefer to distance themselves from women who were technically committing a 'sinful' act by not wearing, or who were viewed as being less pious on the basis of not wearing the *hijab*. Also as an extension of this idea, would they use the *hijab* to distance themselves from non-Muslims as well?

Most of the full-time wearers indicated that the main reason why most of their closest friends also wore the *hijab* full-time was not because they viewed non-wearers as impure but instead because of lifestyle reasons.

> Since I wear the *tudung*, I have become more selective of my friends. I become closer to those who follow Islam. They also do what the religion teaches you, what God requires you to do. So to me, if I go with those who do not understand the religion, then it will be difficult to be with them. They might do things which upset me, or I might 'bother' them if I talk about religion. I don't think they are necessarily bad people, but me and them? We will be too different in outlook. We won't have much in common. So that's why most of my friends are wearers.
>
> (Engineering sales executive, 46, married)

I think why I have more close [female Muslim] friends who also wear the *tudung* is because we have the same mindset and same lifestyle. We probably have more in common, like for example, the type of places we prefer to go, and places we prefer not to go. Me and my friends don't like to go discos or parties, for example. So I don't think it is because I think the non-wearers are sinful; no, maybe they're not. But they just don't have so much in common with me.

(Undergraduate, 22, single)

The opposite also appeared to be true, as those who currently were not full-time wearers, tended to report that 'most' of their close female Muslim friends were also non-wearers. Yet, their rationale was not directly connected with being pious per se, but again in connection with issues of lifestyle.

I think I don't click with them very well … I do have a few good friends [who are full-time wearers], but I wouldn't say that they are my closest friends. I think the *tudung* girls like to go to the mosque, or discuss religion, or go religious classes. My [female Muslim] friends are less like that. We do other things, go other places together.

(Undergraduate, 23, single)

One respondent who was a full-time *hijab* wearer, who graduated from the *madrasah* education system and furthered her studies at an Islamic tertiary institution abroad gave a slightly different reason for the predominance of full-time wearer friends as opposed to non-wearers.

From young, all my close friends wore the *hijab*; this is probably because I went to a *madrasah*, and all the girls there also were full-time wearers. And so, I suppose that my whole social circle were *hijabis*. So therefore most of my closest friends are also wearers. I never had much opportunity to get to know non-wearers well.

(Full-time private tutor, 22, married)

When specifically asked about their views on being in the presence of their female Muslim friends who exposed the *aurat*, most respondents indicated some discomfort, but not rejection or anger. Most of the respondents also claimed not to be prejudiced against 'non-wearers'.

A bit 'not nice' feeling [when with non-wearers] but what they wear – or don't wear – is really not my business. They can be nice people, or we might have to work with them. So, there's no point in getting upset or angry. I just focus on myself.

(Postgraduate research student, 23, single)

I see non-wearers, or I stand near them, no big deal. Muslim non-wearers, non-Muslims; it doesn't matter to me. What matters is 'me' and 'myself' [emphasis original]. What they [non-wearers] do, has no effect on me. I need to be sincere to myself.

(Teacher, 31, married)

It was also noticeable that all ten full-time *hijab* wearers interviewed did have a few close female Muslim friends who were not 'full-time wearers' or 'non-wearers'.

Most of my closest female Muslim friends also wear the *tudung* full time. But my best friend does not currently wear. I don't pressure her; she doesn't talk about wearing to me, except once when she said she will wear when she's ready. She's a good girl, at heart. So being with her – a non-wearer – doesn't affect me at all.

(Teacher, 23, single)

It was interesting that most respondents claimed that the *hijab* was not necessarily the key marker which the pious Muslim woman employs to distance herself from the less pious. Rather they claimed that behaviour – referring to whether or not certain actions were appropriate – was much more important as a factor.

Actually, I believe it is possible to be modest without necessarily wearing the *hijab*. And it is therefore also possible that a person who wears the *hijab* might not be acting modestly. Both are possible. However, what is therefore the most important thing is that the woman behaves modestly.

(Civil servant, 23, single, non-wearer)

At the same time, most respondents indicated that the *hijab* served as an accepted marker for setting appropriate social distance between the self and others, especially in public.

I feel that in Singapore, most people understand what the *tudung* represents. It tells others that I am a chaste and modest woman. So no need to spell it out for them, they can see. And they treat me accordingly. For example, I won't shake hands with men I don't know, even at work. But the men they also know, so they don't expect me to shake their hands. Maybe except the foreigner ... he might not know.

(Full-time private tutor, 23, married)

When asked about wearing the *hijab* in public, most respondents reported that they did not face significant social obstacles. Most wearers claimed that they did not feel Singaporean employers discriminated negatively against *hijab* wearers. Non-wearers also reported that their choice not to wear the *hijab* was not dictated by their career.

Maybe you heard stories of bosses not wanting to hire *tudung* women because they say these women won't do this, won't do that. I do not know how true this story is, my boss is not like this, and I do not know anyone who experienced this. I feel the *tudung* in Singapore – outside of the school issue – is not an issue.

(Journalist, 23, single, non-wearer)

Although the respondents who were full-time wearers in this study suggested that they did not have a problem wearing the *hijab* to work and that they interacted normally with Muslim women who were non-wearers, as well as non-Muslims, there have been cases whereby wearers do face pressure from potential employers to forego the *hijab* (*Singapore Straits Times*, 29 September 2002). In addition, there are still quite a number of vocations in the civil service, such as professions in nursing and in the police force that disallow Muslim women wearing the *hijab*. In the light of this, it is plausible to assume that the wearers' smooth transition into the workplace includes rejecting jobs that are problematic when it comes to wearing the *hijab*. As such, there is a form of mild enclavement both externally and internally imposed on Muslim women towards particular kinds of jobs.

However, some respondents indicated that 'the public' understood the *hijab* and its meanings, as illustrated by this brief anecdote.

I guess the public understand the meaning of the *tudung* for me. For example, I wouldn't be invited onto stage for some types of performance, even if it is just for the students. They [colleagues] understand I would not feel comfortable. So they don't ask, I don't have to decline; it's understood.

(Teacher, 31, married)

Some have even mentioned that they get 'extra' space in certain environments, because people understand that proximity might be an issue for the *hijab* wearer.

For example, sometimes we have no choice but to be on a crowded train or bus, but people seem to give me more space. Or maybe I just think they are giving me more space. Doesn't matter; I am quite comfortable knowing I have space. I don't see it as them avoiding me. More likely it is that they understand. Well, perhaps not all the time, but sometimes.

(Graduate student, 23, single)

In this sense, it is evident that the *hijab*, as a visible symbol of, not just Muslim identity but also piety, draws up 'rules of engagement'. Those who seem to understand the *hijab* tend to accept its enclavement strategy by giving the wearer more 'space'. However, by giving this space, despite the distance, the mutual understanding and acceptance benefits the relationship as both parties are accommodated.

Nevertheless the respondents made clear that non-Muslims who 'understand' the *hijab* were in the minority. This anecdote from a non-wearer gave an insight into what might cross the mind of non-Muslims that do not understand the *hijab*.

Sometimes, people ask me why those who wear the *tudung* are so unfriendly, don't socialize, don't do a lot of things. They won't go ask those Muslims, they ask me. I can explain. I think they dare not ask [the wearers] because they are afraid of asking, or maybe they are afraid that the *tudung* wearers all terrorists. They [non-Muslims] have no clue.

(Financial analyst, 21, single, non-wearer)

When I first wore the *hijab* full-time, my boss wanted to speak to me. He asked if this [wearing] meant anything. I just said it meant I wanted to be a better Muslim. He then asked if my wearing the *hijab* would affect my work, who I met, or if I have to go to the back room. I said nothing else needs to change. So we went back to normal, and after time, I think it doesn't cross my boss' mind anymore that I wear the *hijab*.

(Sales engineer, 46, married)

We have found that the *hijab* is a central aspect of religious life for pious Muslim women in Singapore. It has become more than a symbol or an identity, but a constitutive part of the self. As Atasoy wrote

Rather than conceptualize the veil as a frozen embodiment of a particular culture or its subversion, women see their veils as symbols of cultural engagement in the struggle for selfhood. This struggle is located within an Islamic cultural ethos, yet it is one in which women connect veiling to their own particular life stories ... veiling operates in a manner that shapes their understanding of themselves. It is anchored in the complex intersection of a claim for cultural adherence to an Islamic moral code of modesty and the quest for self-assertion.

(Atasoy, 2006: 218–9)

By becoming one with the self, the *hijab* distances the pious self from the profane and mundane world. With the boundaries clearly drawn, the pious can now securely navigate without fear of losing their religiosity.

Interpersonal relationships

The final stop on our journey to understand social distancing and the maintenance of purity was at the body itself. More specifically, we sought to understand the significance of religion on how pious Muslims formed and maintained interpersonal relationships such as friendships or marriages. In simple terms, an individual will have different levels of interpersonal relationships. At the furthest level, individuals might have an 'economic' relationship, that is, relationships involving instrumental transactions between two people. They only interact because they 'have to', not because they 'want to'. In Furnivall's sense, a plural society is one where various groups only have economic relations, and very little social relations, with each other. Social relations, in our sense, refer to friendships, at one end of the social scale, and marriage, at the other end. Friendships are broadly defined as long-term reciprocal and personal relationships between individuals that are based on common interest or outlook (Allan, 1989). Marriage, at the other end of the scale, is perhaps the ultimate form of friendship, as it is a formally recognized long-term relationship between two people, who are so close that they engage in sexual relations with each other, not just for the purposes of reproduction but also for other reasons (Allan, 1989).

As mentioned earlier, would an individual's piety influence his or her choice of, at one level, friends and at another level, spouse? Already, we have discussed the notion of religious purity and contamination. To remain pious is to remain religiously pure and to avoid contamination. It therefore could be posited that friendships with people of a different religion, who might have practices and mindsets that are in conflict with Islam, might be viewed as being 'dangerous' and therefore are to be avoided. As such, the 'safest' strategy would be to only befriend those of the same religion, and by extension of the same level of piety. Also, it could be argued that a pious person might also choose to only marry someone of the same religion, as a strategy to maintain purity and piety. Marrying someone of the same religion is an act of homogamy or endogamy, even though the term also refers to the practice of seeking marriage partners who are similar in ethnicity, or socio-economic status. On the one hand, homogamy and endogamy encourage group affiliation and bonding, as those who are already socially and culturally alike are brought closer together through marriage. On the other hand, it does not contribute to wider social cohesion in the larger society. In this sense, homogamy is the ultimate act of social enclavement, because insiders are welcomed and embraced while outsiders are kept out.

As one might expect, there are many different types of homogamy, based on ethnicity, socio-economic status and so on. For religious homogamy, Heaton and Pratt (1990) have put forward the proposal that marrying a person of the same religion would build marital satisfaction and stability. Lazerwitz (1981) suggests that if religious homogamy is maintained, then it is less likely to end in divorce. In both cases, the sharing of religious values is assumed to be critical in holding marriages together. Yet, perhaps the most important reason why some individuals seek to practise religious homogamy is to maintain their religious purity. In other words, religious homogamy could be the ultimate form of voluntary enclavement. The question, as far as this research is concerned, was whether Singapore Muslims practised religious homogamy, and by association, some form of social distancing? Again, Singapore served as an interesting test case, because Muslims constitute a numerical minority within the population. Thus, it follows that there is a relatively small pool of potential Muslim spouses, while there is correspondingly a much larger pool of potential non-Muslim spouses. Furthermore, as the society is (in theory) multicultural and multiracial – in the sense that there is state-ordered 'integration' and 'interaction' among the races – then the possibility arises that individuals might, initially, form friendships, and later, potentially 'fall in love' with someone of another religion. We wanted to ask if pious Muslims would then take the next step and marry a non-Muslim?

In the Social Distance Project, we asked the 30 'middle-class' respondents to talk about their 'close friends'. The general findings are summarized in Table 6.1. On this basis, we noted that our sample of self-described 'pious' Muslims did not exclusively have friends who were Muslims. Instead, all of them reported that they

Table 6.1 Findings on friends and friendship (N = 30)

View	Response (%)
My closest friend ...	
... is also a Muslim	28 (93%)
... is as religious or more religious than myself	15 (50%)
... is of the same gender as well	27 (90%)
... is from the same age group (plus/minus 5 years of age)	29 (96%)
Of my 10 closest friends ...	
... all are Muslims	3 (10%)
... more than half are Muslims	25 (83.33%)
... less than half are Muslims	2 (6.66%)
... none are Muslims	0

had close friends who were from other races, ethnic groups or religious affiliations. It was not surprising that for most, their closest friend was a Muslim; after all, friendships are based on common interests and outlook. This point is reinforced given that for most, their 'closest friend' was also of the same gender, and was from the same age group. What was also interesting was that many respondents commented that it was 'unrealistic' that Muslims in Singapore had exclusively Muslim friends. Many were at pains to stress that Singapore was a multiracial society, and Muslims could be good friends with people of any religion or race.

What was more interesting was that exactly half reported that their closest friend was 'less religious' than the respondent. When asked to elaborate, several respondents were able to articulate exactly their difference in religiosity. For example, one respondent said that his best friend was not so 'disciplined' about aspects such as praying five times a day, or was rather 'careless' when dining in public. However, those that indicated that their best friends were 'less religious', were quick to stress that they did not judge or 'preach'. Most said that they would just value the friendship, and leave issues of religiosity to the other person. It was, as many said, a very personal affair. Already, we had noted that many women respondents who wore the *hijab* reported that they were perfectly comfortable being close friends, or being in the company, of other Muslim women who were not wearing the *hijab*.

For the two respondents – both male – whose best friend was not a Muslim, they said that their difference in religious affiliation was never an issue. One respondent, whose best friend was Christian Chinese, said that their 20-year friendship was not only based on their common interests such as football but also based on mutual respect. The other respondent, whose best friend was Indian and Hindu, reported that they were working at the same organization, which probably strengthened their friendship.

Marriage

While our research found that Muslims did not treat sharing religious affiliation as a prerequisite for forming close friendships, when it came to marriage, religion was of paramount importance. All respondents who participated in the Social Distance

Project said that they would only marry Muslims. There would be no exceptions. However, their reasons for this choice proved interesting.

> Islam is not [just] my way of life; it is my life. Everything must be done in God's way, the Islamic way. This therefore also includes marriage and having children. They must also be Muslim. There isn't another way.
>
> (Civil servant, female, 23, single)

Another emergent strand from the interviews was that many of these respondents 'never considered' or 'never entertained' the thought of marrying people from other religions.

> Marrying someone from another religion never really crossed my mind. I am committed to Islam. I want my husband to also be committed to Islam. And my children will be committed to Islam. So, really, never an option.
>
> (Journalist, female, 23, single)

In this sense, it was already clear that some sort of social distancing had been active, because their mental processes already adopted a pre-judgement by only entertaining Muslim persons as possible partners, while non-Muslims were never considered. This therefore led to a situation where the dilemma of marrying a non-Muslim spouse did not arise, at least in their imagination.

> I have no qualms about marrying someone of another ethnic group so long he is Muslim. Although I know that my mother will prefer me to marry a pious Muslim man. The reason being, she is not sure if she skeptical if the person is converting just for the sake of marriage or whether he really believes in Islam.
>
> (Caterer, Female, 50s, married)

We also asked the men in the study about their views on marrying someone of a different religion. The responses from the men were exactly the same as those from the women.

> I will consider somebody [Muslim] from a different ethnic group, but it's a definite 'no' to people of different religious groups unless the person converts.
>
> (Manager, male, 29, married)

> Different ethnic group, yes. I don't see any problems. Preference, no. My parents will preference for ethnic groups, though … the Malays. Different religious group, no. Unless the person converts. If they convert because of marriage, my answer is still no. Islam doesn't allow. They must be a Muslim because they believe in Islam. This will translate into problems later with the children. In Indonesia we can see this a lot, civil marriages for example amongst pop stars.
>
> (Teacher, male, 28, single)

Thus, despite the stereotypical liberal attitudes that middle-class men and women are supposed to have, those in our sample felt that it was still imperative to marry a Muslim spouse. This trend towards homogamy between Muslims emerged despite the fact that these middle-class Muslims are among the better educated strata and are therefore in workplaces where they are very likely to meet other middle-class people with whom they share common tastes. This common denominator might include common values, aspirations, interests and lifestyles. Yet, since these respondents insisted that they would only expect non-Muslims to convert into Islam first before considering marriage, this suggests that for the middle-class respondents in this study religious considerations override social class similarities.

Furthermore, we found from the interviews that conversion by itself was not an automatic guarantee for agreeing to marry. Put in another way, some of our respondents were still wary about the religious status of converts into Islam. Here are some views of respondents who were asked to hypothetically consider marrying someone who had already converted into Islam.

> I will be hesitant [to marry] even if that person converts to Islam, because I'm not sure whether I will be able to guide him well. And with the kids, it will be quite difficult. You will have to nurture them Islamically, I mean, mostly on your own. There will be little support in that sense from the spouse. So I will still prefer to marry a [born] Muslim.
>
> (Homemaker, female, 50s, married)

> Has the person really converted or not? If say a non-Muslim [potential spouse] were to be interested in me, I would ask myself if he'll be embracing the religion because he wants to marry me or because he really believes in Islam. If it is the latter, then yes, I would consider marrying him. If it's the former, I could consider, after all, if that is the way God has laid for him to discover the religion, then who are we to judge? But I would not rush into it.
>
> (Manager, female, 26)

We also asked respondents for their views on marrying people of a different ethnicity or race. We found that by and large religion was still the key factor. In other words, they would in theory marry an Indian or an Arab as long as they were Muslims. They would even marry people who were from races or ethnicities such as the Chinese or Americans that were not commonly associated with Islam, if they again converted into Islam.

> I have no preference with regard to the individual's ethnic group. I will not compromise on the religious aspect. I will not marry him unless he converts to Islam.
>
> (Assistant manager, female, 24, single)

> I have no preference when it comes to the person's ethnic group. But I will definitely not marry someone from a different religious group. Not unless they convert to Islam.
>
> (IT executive, male, 29, married)

In Singapore, there are statistics on inter-ethnic marriages and interestingly religion was a key factor for some of these. Between 1967 and 1970, 14.5 per cent of Christian and 12.7 per cent of Muslim marriages were inter-ethnic; these rates were much higher than the overall inter-ethnic marriage rate of 5.25 per cent for 1962–1968 (Hassan and Benjamin, 1973). The main explanation for this phenomenon was that Christianity and Islam as religions were more likely to have peoples of different ethnicities, as opposed to Chinese religions (such as Taoism and traditional Chinese ancestor worship) and Hinduism in Singapore, which remain largely embedded in the Chinese and Indian communities respectively. Hassan (1971) argued that Muslims and Christians in Singapore were far more likely to override ethnic considerations, and these two religions were avenues of ethnic assimilation. Between 1962 and 1969, 25 per cent of inter-marriages were between Malays and Indians, and 18 per cent of inter-marriages were between Chinese and Malays (Hassan and Benjamin, 1973). Another study, done by Lee (1988), covering the periods 1965–1980, found that inter-ethnic marriages were more frequent within the Muslims in Singapore, with more than one in ten Muslim marriages involving partners of different ethnic backgrounds (Lee, 1988: 258). More recently, a newspaper report documented that there were more inter-ethnic group marriages than before, especially among Muslims. Inter-ethnic marriages increased from 6.5 per cent in 1996 to 13.7 per cent in 2006 for non-Muslim marriages and for Muslim marriages in the same period, the increase was from 20.5 per cent to 29.7 per cent. While inter-ethnic marriages made up 9 per cent of marriages in 1980, the number had increased to 17 per cent by the year 2000 (*Singapore Straits Times*, 17 December 2001).

However, given that census statistics have not shown Malays who profess other religions – that is a Malay person who indicates that he or she is a Christian, Taoist or Hindu – it is safe to assume that most of the inter-ethnic marriages involving Malays, 99.1 per cent of whom are Muslim, involved conversion into Islam. Another explanation for the higher rate of Indian-Malay inter-marriages is that there exists a fairly large and long-standing Indian-Muslim community in Singapore. Also, there were unlikely to be many cases of Malays marrying out into another religion, as the percentage of Muslims has always remained the same. We found that the reasons behind the 'one-way' traffic mentality – where the only option was conversion into Islam and not vice versa – were not examples of religious xenophobia, racism or ethnocentrism, but instead a deep-seated desire to maintain religiosity or piety.

> I really got nothing against any other religion. Live and let live. But you cannot ask me to live my life under any other religion. It is impossible. Islam is my religion. Islam is my life. If I cannot find a person who shares this same view, I will not be so desperate as to leave Islam, just to get married. No, I would rather stay single and Muslim.
>
> (Civil servant, male, 37, married)

However, it is imperative to recognize that within Singapore's Muslim community some enclavement continues to occur, mainly on the basis of one's ethnicity and religious ideology. This finding is quite contrary to some literature on the 'collapsible' nature of Malay identity. For example, there exists the phrase *masuk Melayu* (which translates into enter into 'Malay-hood') if one converts into Islam and subsequently adopts an Islamic name (Purushotam, 1998: 151–153). While this phrase is more commonly used in Malaysia, it was only sparingly used in Singapore. However, historical ethnic prejudices and stereotypes within the Muslim community can still be seen in the everyday life of Singaporean Muslims. Historically, authors such as Djamour (1965), Abdullah (1959) and Abdul Aziz (1962) have contributed works on the various segments of the Malay/Muslim community in Singapore, drawing attention to the hostilities between some Malay/Muslims against non-Malay/Muslims. For example, there were movements to differentiate between the Darah Keturunan Arab (DKA) (translated: Those of Arab Descent) and Darah Keturunan Keling (DKK) (translated: Those of Indian Descent) (Djamour, 1965: 220, 245). Abdul Aziz Johari's work also documented the cultural differences and antagonisms between the Javanese and Bawean sub-communities (Abdul Aziz, 1962). From anecdotal evidence, some of these ethnic divisions still exist within the larger Singaporean Muslim community today.

At the same time, Mariam Mohamed Ali (1989) and Kamaludeen (2007a) have also documented how Muslims in Singapore are fractured along different ideological dimensions. Thus, marital stability and conflict are not just based on religious homogamy. What is also of paramount importance is the degree to which Muslim couples agree on specific religious issues – such as the degree of piety or their joint commitment to the religious practices – even within same-faith marriages. This was borne out in our study, when respondents said that they also would not marry anyone just because the potential spouse was Muslim. Compatibility of views, including religious views, was important.

Our research on marriage has nevertheless shown several trends. Pious Muslims prioritize remaining faithful to the tenets of Islam over and above any other consideration. In other words, most respondents said that they would rather remain unmarried than have to convert into another religion. On the one hand, this might appear to be an example of social distancing: Muslims refuse to 'come out'. On the other hand, the degree at which Muslims welcome those who want to 'convert in' appears to be fairly high. If Muslims accept converts as (almost) being the same as born Muslims, then it can be argued that the door is always open. As such, this is not total social distancing.

Conclusion

Our examination of veiling, more accurately modest dressing for Muslim women, and views towards interpersonal relationships, have yielded interesting results. It has shown that because the religious purity of the body is at stake, pious Muslims will not compromise on the issue of marriage. For them, there will always be a distance between themselves and the non-believer. This distance can be close friendships, but it cannot evolve further into physical intimate relations. That pious Muslims might consider marriage to converts into Islam does suggest that race and ethnicity are not obstacles; the only obstacle is religion. In this sense, the act of piety, for Muslims, is to remain religiously pure by only marrying other Muslims.

The issue of the *hijab* is slightly more complicated. Although a mandatory religious requirement, its use in Singapore is less straightforward. Part of the reason for the complication is because the state has a policy which disallows the wearing of the *hijab* in national schools; as such, a unique situation is created in which pious Muslim women are denied the opportunity to practise an act of piety for some hours of the day. We found that this situation has led many pious Muslim women to re-interpret this act of piety as being a rite of passage, and a test of their own religiosity. At the same time, this act of piety can be interpreted by the public as a distancing device, as the *hijab* clearly signals to the public that these Muslim women are pious. However, in Singapore, wearing the *hijab* does not appear to be exclusionist but like dining and *halal* consciousness, it is a defensive strategy that allows them and the non-Muslims to engage with each other, albeit with the 'ground rules' clearly established. In sum, the acts of piety with regard to the body do not appear to be malicious forms of social distancing or enclavement.

7 Conclusion

State, enclaves and religion

Managing and enclaving religions

Our central argument has been that the Singaporean state, since achieving independence in 1965, has been active in creating policies to manage the Muslim community. These policies have been, from the political elite's point of view, largely successful in incorporating the Muslim community, suppressing radical movements and avoiding overt racial conflict. The Singaporean experience may well have relevance for other societies in the region such as China and a degree of relevance beyond Asia. There is some anecdotal evidence that the Chinese authorities are following the Singapore way in regarding religion as potentially part of the rich tapestry of Chinese culture and a useful source of foreign currency when its sites and pilgrimages can attract foreign tourist interest. For instance, Taoist sites at Wudang mountain in China are slowly emerging as part of the new commercial order by attracting pilgrims, including overseas Chinese (DeBernardi, 2008). However, converting religion into a tourist attraction can only be successful if religious expression and recruitment are carefully managed. In developing this idea of the 'management of religions', we have examined the implicit and explicit policies of containment, or enclavement as we call it, and the more positive policy of 'upgrading' of Muslims in order to manage them more effectively. The Singapore elite is obviously conscious of the revival and growth of Islam in the region and is concerned with maintaining control of its own Muslim community. Islam is inevitably associated with the 'Malay problem' and part of the state's religious policy is to incorporate Muslims into its vision of a technological, rational, consumer society through paternalist strategies of education, training and improvement. As we have seen, one aspect of this strategy is to modernize *madrasah* education in both content and orientation. More broadly, these state policies and institutions include:

- State management of Islam in Singapore (AMLA, *Syariah* law, MUIS, mosques, and religious leadership);
- 'Upgrading', through the education system, public housing, legislation, the National Service, self-help groups and the group representation constituency (GRC) electoral system;

- Defusing crises, such as the 9/11 and JI issue, and managing the possible impact on community relations in Singapore; and
- State management of the predominantly Muslim working class.

More recently, there has been an attempt to promote Singapore as the regional hub of religious dialogue and inter-faith harmony that is a model of the successful bureaucratic management of diversity; for example, the Singapore Islamic Hub on Braddell Road not only houses MUIS headquarters, the *Madrasah* Al-Irsyad and the Muhajirin Mosque, but is planned as a learning and inter-faith nexus (*Singapore Straits Times*, 29 May 2005). Since 2005, the Hub has established a post-graduate Islamic studies programme with the Al-Azhar Islamic University of Cairo (*Singapore Straits Times*, 8 May 2005) as well as inter-faith dialogue programmes with the Hartford Seminary from the USA (*Singapore Straits Times*, 26 September 2006). The government wants to advertise its planning successes, to function as an example of harmony in the region and to emerge as a global city state.

In comparative terms, religious diversity has, with the collapse of communism and the rise of fundamentalism, become a major political issue in the majority of democratic liberal societies, which have in general been slow to develop effective social policies and institutions to manage the social tensions that flow from such cultural complexity (Turner, 2006c). Many of the conventional liberal solutions that embraced a rather simple model of secularism no longer appear to be wholly relevant. In this study of Singapore, we have considered one particular community against a more general background of increasingly difficult problems of multiculturalism and religious diversity in relation to the state and the law, especially after the international crisis created by the terrorist acts of 9/11, and the bombings in Bali, London and Madrid. The governments of advanced societies can no longer rely on the simple institutional divisions between politics and religion, and have entered into a new phase that involves the direct management of religions. Liberal states have evolved from utilizing policies of benign neglect to active management of religious activities. In practice, these new strategies are primarily concerned with managing Muslims under the banner of pluralism and multiculturalism.

These developments can be understood in terms of the concept of governmentality, since managing religions is a recent adjunct of the more general functions of the administrative state (Foucault, 2000). Managing religions is politically important, if the state is to re-assert its authority over society, and especially over those religious institutions that seek to articulate an alternative vision of power and truth. If the state is to command the loyalty of its citizens over and above the claims of religious membership and identity, it needs to build up forms of social solidarity that can successfully embrace a variety of religious traditions. We do not pretend that solutions to social diversity in modern civil societies are easy to find or enact, especially where different religious traditions claim to possess different versions of the truth. A further complication occurs where religions are themselves *internally* divided for example between *Sunni* and *Shi'ite* traditions. The current divisions within the Anglican Communion over homosexuality would be another illustration. In these cases, the critical issue is political: who has the authority to speak on behalf of a whole community?

In our account of these processes, we have broadly distinguished two forms of management or governmentality of religions. The first is the rational model and its variants that constitute what we have called a strategy of upgrading religions. A second policy involves the isolation and containment of separate communities. This second option is not unlike Furnivall's notion of plural society (1956) as a reflection on Burma. Furnivall argued that in many Asian societies with multiple ethnic communities, these social groups lived separate social lives, meeting only in the market place for exchange. In this study we have argued that one solution to modern security problems has been to encourage or tolerate the enclavement of social groups, especially minorities. In our study, we have noted that enclavement can be either a direct policy objective or the unintended consequence of religious revivalism. The dominant strategy in Singapore has been to upgrade Islam, but a secondary aspect of the religious field is the division of society into racial groups – Chinese, Hindu, Malay and others – which largely correspond to religious differences. Thus, Singapore's multiracial policy necessarily divides the population by religion, thereby creating enclaves. These separate socio-religious groups are further consolidated into enclaves as the unintended consequence of religious revivalism and personal piety.

With respect to the Muslim community, these policies tend to assume that Islam has to be modernized if it is to be compatible with a secular political regime. This is in fact the policy of creating so-called 'moderate Muslims'. The strategies that are involved here include educational policies to raise the educational level of Muslim communities, including providing educational improvement of Muslim leaders, especially the *Ustazs*. It also involves providing legislation to give Muslim women security, opportunities in education, and encouragement to enter the open marriage market, thereby rejecting arranged marriages. It may also involve inducements to abandon the veil or other forms of modesty and seclusion. Finally these forms of government intervention also involve opposition to what are seen to be brutal criminal law decisions, such as amputation. In short, the liberal management of religion is intended to modernize religion through a set of procedures that bring about a partial secularization of society. Although the majority of pious Muslims would probably regard these strategies as deeply problematic because they appear to change the nature of personal piety, a small group of modernists might themselves welcome such strategies. These liberal policies may well be compatible for example with the modernizing thought of the Iranian philosopher Abdolkarim Soroush (Sadri and Sadri, 2000).

When we ask the question: 'Who has the authority to speak on behalf of a community?', the notion of the religious elite becomes very problematic. Who gets to define who the religious elite are? However, measures to institutionalize and formalize those to whom the titles of *ustazs* and *ustazahs* can be accredited are underway 'to remedy' this situation. Religious teachers will now go on the Asatizah Recognition Scheme (*Singapore Straits Times*, 29 December 2005; 9 January 2006). It goes beyond the voluntary self-registration for *asatizah* that was introduced in 2002. The new scheme will allow only registered teachers to be called *ustaz,* for men, and *ustazah,* for women. The board is made up of *Ustaz* Ali Mohamed, chairman of the Khadijah Mosque who chairs the eight-member board. It includes: *Ustaz* Mohamad Rais, president of the *Syariah* Court, *Ustaz* Mohamad Hasbi Hassan, president of PERGAS, and *Ustaz* Pasuni Maulan, chairman of the *Madrasah* Aljunied management committee. Those who are rejected can appeal to a three-member panel chaired by the *Mufti,* Syed Isa Semait. However, this form of accreditation is not universally accepted in Singapore with a number of religious elites feeling displaced and dispossessed. Even though some of these elites do not have 'paper qualifications', they do exert a significant amount of influence in the Muslim community. Freelance preacher *Ustaz* Ahmad Dahri wanted the scheme to recognize teachers with experience but without the required qualifications. 'Recognition by the wider community is a form of recognition as well. It is a good certificate too' (*Singapore Straits Times,* 29 December 2005). Popular freelance preacher *Ustaz* Fahrurazi Kiayi Kassim, who lacks formal religious qualifications but is currently taking a diploma course run by PERGAS and Perdaus, hoped that being recognized will reduce apprehension that others may have towards him (*Singapore Straits Times,* 29 December 2005). A president of a Muslim social organization here retorted with indignation about who gave these *asatizahs* the right to proclaim themselves *ulamas*? He continued that even those so called *ulamas* from PERGAS can attempt to instruct society in the incorrect teachings of Islam (Kamaludeen, 2007b). These 'debates' suggest that state-appointed religious elites do not automatically become accepted by the ordinary Muslim.

Syed Isa Semait, an Arab Muslim, is Singapore's *Mufti.* He has held office for over three decades. In a book published by MUIS, the *Mufti* has been likened to an institution in the Singapore Muslim community (Zuraidah, 1994). There are claims that his religious pronouncements are sometimes dictated by the government. To which he said: 'In all my twenty-two years I can safely say that the government has never interfered in my work or given me any direction. People will say what they will' (Zuraidah, 1994: 69). He proudly says that the government has done well in protecting the Muslims' identity and interests (Zuraidah, 1994). The position of the Singapore *Mufti* is a peculiarity unto itself. He is a member of the religious elite, complete with a degree from Al Azhar Islamic University of Cairo; yet, within the setup of a secular state, he is positioned in an institution/organization created by the state whereby the highest authority of the statutory board is the President who is a government bureaucrat, a civil servant. The *Mufti* plays a pivotal role in the disciplining of Islam in Singapore. Touted by the state as the highest authority on Islam (*Singapore Straits Times,* 7 February 2002), he is well placed within the hierarchy to take on the task of normalizing judgements. However, there are obvious tensions when the *Mufti* declares on the one hand that the *hijab* need not be worn by girls while attending national schools, while simultaneously declaring on the other hand that it is a religious obligation for girls to wear the *hijab.*

The *Mufti* is located within MUIS, which was established as a statutory body in 1968 under sections 87 and 88 of the AMLA, to oversee the development and progress of *madrasah* education. The MUIS and the *Mufti* are given their legislative and disciplinary powers by the AMLA. Under the AMLA, the MUIS is to advise the President of Singapore on all matters relating to Islam in Singapore. Amongst the principal functions of the MUIS is the issuance of *fatwas*. Although these institutional ties might give state officials significant leverage over the religious scholarly community, most in the religious community managed to escape state control (Kamaludeen and Aljunied, 2009).

If bureaucratic management through upgrading Islam is a conscious and explicit policy, the more repressive strategy of containment through the creation of enclaves is often the unintended consequence of earlier attitudes of neglect or indifference. The history of British race relations shows a relatively long period of benign neglect that has been followed in recent years by intense government intervention to encourage and to promote moderate Islam. Ironically the leadership of the Christian churches in the United Kingdom has complained that the new emphasis on Islam has been biased and unbalanced, leading to the neglect of the Christian contribution to society.

In a criticism of much contemporary globalization theory which assumes the emergence of porous social borders, modern society is becoming an enclave society in which various practices including the creation of ghettoes and no-go areas produce strategies of social and cultural quarantine. If the first strategy is one of upgrading, the second is a strategy of containment through the development of social enclaves. The word 'enclave' comes from the Latin for key (*clavis*) and therefore to enclave a community is to lock it up, but the modern enclave is not simply a walled society; there are many new technologies available to governments whereby they can exercise surveillance and control without obvious physical barriers. We might speculate that enclavement is a strategy that may be adopted when upgrading policies appear to have already failed or for political reasons are made to fail. After 9/11 domestic security requiring the close surveillance of the population has increasingly become the dominant concern and liberal upgrading policies have been subject to political criticism because they are thought to be 'soft on terrorism'.

The liberal vision of consensus

Given the global development of religious revivalism and religious nationalism, new political questions have emerged about how states can best manage pluralism, religious diversity and ethnic divisions. The classic liberal solution has been presented by John Rawls in his *The Law of Peoples* (2001) where he argues that a 'decent liberal society' will require 'an overlapping consensus' in which social order must be rooted in a reasonable political conception of right and where political harmony is reinforced by an overlapping consensus of comprehensive doctrines. In attempting to provide the classical liberal defence of freedom of speech and conscience, Rawls confronts the traditional problem that some religious fundamentalists or political groups may not accept the liberal version of an open plural society. How does a liberal properly respond to somebody or group which simply rejects the principles of liberal tolerance? Rawls provides no real practical solution to this conventional conundrum. In historical terms in response to the carnage of religious conflict in the seventeenth century, liberalism solved religious conflict by making religion a matter of private belief, separating church and state and developing the rule of law. These political solutions were initially expressed in John Locke's 'Letter on tolerance' which was composed in 1667 and in *The Second Treatise of Government* in 1690 (Locke, 1946). Locke's principles of liberal government – government by consent, the responsibility of government for the welfare of the community, the church as voluntary association, the limitation of the power of magistrates, and the rule of law – became the basis of liberalism for at least two centuries. Perhaps the limitation of Locke's individualism is that he did not fully recognize the binding power of social ties, especially of race, religion and ethnicity, and his notion of tolerance was essentially tolerance within the Christian community rather than between religions of very different constituent theologies and institutions.

Because ethnic and religious conflicts in the modern world are exacerbated by globalization, social philosophers have turned to the question of how tolerance and cosmopolitanism might be promoted. These philosophical debates have created a rich stream of theories and concepts – cosmopolitan virtue, care, tolerance and recognition ethics. Although these ideas are useful in the formulation of ethical orientations, they do not easily or immediately lead to empirical research strategies or to effective social policies. The work of Will Kymlicka has become important in addressing the issue of rights in ethnically diverse societies through the notion of group rights.

Kymlicka (1995) has promoted the idea of group rights and cultural rights within a liberal framework (as a policy that has specific reference to multicultural societies such as Canada and Australia). Kymlicka argues that liberal democracies that have accepted some form of multiculturalism typically make adjustments or accommodations to cultural pluralism through the mechanism of what he calls 'group-differentiated rights' (1995: 26). These are divided into three types. First, there are rights to self-government. In multinational states, the component nations may demand some level of political autonomy or territorial jurisdiction. The right of self-determination has been sanctioned by the United Nations' Charter – 'all peoples have a right to self-determination' – but the charter does not unfortunately define 'people'. In some societies, the demand for autonomy may result in secession, but one common institutional response to the demand for autonomy has been federalism. In some respects, Kymlicka's argument may therefore be specific to Canada, where federalism has offered some solution to the demands of the Quebecois for autonomy. The second accommodation is through the development of poly-ethnic rights. At a minimal level, these are merely rights to express cultural differences without exposure to harassment and prejudice. These rights are often expressed against so-called 'Anglo-conformity' which has involved the dominance of Anglo-American values in the public domain, relegating other cultural practices to the private sphere. More radical demands for these rights may entail the exemption of ethnic groups from laws and regulations that are seen to discriminate against them.

As a federal and as a white-settler society, Canada has first-nation communities with a problematic relationship to the history and sovereignty of the Canadian state. The point of these rights is to promote social integration, whereas self-government rights are designed to secure self-government. Finally there are special representation rights in which minority or oppressed groups are given automatic representation in parliamentary and other democratic institutions. While these rights can be regarded as a form of affirmative action, they tend to be temporary. They are 'kick-start' devices to ensure some development towards adequate participation and they are subsequently abandoned once minority or marginalized groups have entered the mainstream of the host community. These rights can therefore be regarded as aspects of the upgrading of cultural minorities.

The theory of differentiated rights, while providing a general legal framework, is in practice specific to Canadian history and society. Some aspects of the argument, however, can apply to Europe, where federalism could be a useful principle of accommodation. In addition, poly-ethnic rights already apply to certain social groups, but not to others. The headscarf issue in French schools is the obvious illustration. However, one criticism of Kymlicka's general approach is the absence of any significant discussion of law. There is no attempt to connect legal pluralism with group-differentiated rights. Kymlicka's rights are in fact primarily cultural rights and hence the problem of legal sovereignty is not adequately addressed and yet the legal framework is a crucial ingredient of social harmony. One consequence of cultural pluralism might therefore be legal pluralism. If legal pluralism is an inevitable consequence of multiculturalism, then Kymlicka's group-differentiated rights are underdeveloped because they do not recognize the importance of legal self-determination. Legal pluralism would thus stretch the assumptions of liberalism to their limits. For example, the right to join or to leave a social group is central to liberalism. But in Islam there are traditional views regarding the right to opt out as being parallel to apostasy and they could not easily permit such arrangements. The notion that individuals can opt out of their own communities is perhaps the most problematic aspect of individual rights. In the case of marginalized groups or minorities, the very survival of their cultures and traditions requires continuity of socialization and transmission – a process that has historically depended on women. Hence, women are typically subject to excessive (and at times brutal) subordination to such group norms.

We can well illustrate some of the issues around the idea of group rights by going back to the illustration of the headscarf or *tudung* in recent public debate in Singapore. The religious elites released a press statement expressing their worry and concern that if issues which are regarded as important by the Muslims such as the '*tudung* issue', which is a specific requirement for Muslim girls who have attained the age of puberty, are not resolved, a section of Singaporean Muslims might become disillusioned with the concept of freedom of religious practices. The term *tudung* needs to be contextualized within Singapore. It is not the veil that covers most of the face. Rather, it is the contemporary Muslim *hijab* or sometimes termed the headscarf, that leaves the face uncovered. Across the world, the *hijab* in recent times has been the subject of much debate. It is a battleground for the armies of those who are out to purify Islam or demonize it, for example in Morocco (Leila, 1994), Tunisia (Charrad, 1998), Iran (Nakanishi, 1998), Turkey (Fischer, 1978), Thailand (Satha-Anand, 2005), and most recently, France. The fear of the veil being used as tool for political upheaval or a point of contention for feminist debates has done much to fuel this sentiment.

Because of the concept of the Muslim *ummah*, happenings in a particular country get picked up by Muslims from other countries. The '*tudung* issue' in Singapore has sparked off many discussions and comments from scholars all over the world. In Malaysia, on 8 February 2002, over 70 students gathered outside the Singapore High Commission in Kuala Lumpur to protest against Singapore's ban on schoolgirls donning the *tudung* (*Singapore Straits Times*, 9 February 2002). Within Singapore, lines were drawn on the '*tudung* issue'. The state branded the Muslims who fought for wearing the *tudung* in national schools as being politically motivated (*Singapore Straits Times*, 3 February 2002). Facing off against them were the Muslim political elites backing the state (*Singapore Straits Times*, 7 February 2002, 9 February 2002). These political elites, who were mostly PAP members of parliament, argued that the protagonists in the issue were misinterpreting Islam. The irony was that the religious elites lent their weight to the protagonists. For example, PERGAS president, Mr Syed Abdillah Ahmad Al-Jufri, commenting on the state refusing to consider the request from the Muslim community to allow the *hijab* to be worn in addition to the uniform, suggested that Singaporeans were now 'inadvertently restricted' from having an opportunity to experience, from young, the true meaning of living and interacting with others of different races and religions (*Singapore Straits Times*, 21 May 2000). Furthermore, members of PERGAS have strongly argued that in the cases of the families of the four school-going children involved in the issue, their action stems from their sincere desire to practise and inculcate moral values in their children rather than seeking to be distinctive, or challenge the political authority of the Singapore government (PERGAS, 2004: 344). Members of the religious elite alleged that the handling of this issue by the state has already caused dissatisfaction and if not resolved amicably and convincingly would lead to mistrust between the various groups implying that the state rhetoric of strengthening social cohesion (amongst the races) is at risk of being seen only as slogan chanting. The members of the religious elite warned against looking at the concern of a minority group just on the basis of numbers with the excuse that the state has to look into the interest and the well-being of the majority (PERGAS, 2004: 337). This might lead to a tyranny of the majority kind of rule whereby members of a parliament, supported by and representing a majority, can pass laws restricting the rights of ethnic and other minorities (Vasil, 2004: 54).

Kymlicka's contribution to liberal theory implies that societies can survive as effective democracies provided they are able to accommodate divergent cultures and identities. Other writers have been more pessimistic about sustaining social order in the face of social diversity. This is because, as a matter of fact, cultural consensus in modern societies is rare: increasing social diversity undermines the cultural homogeneity of traditional societies. Cooperation with social norms affects attitudes towards how other people will cooperate, and in turn this expectation shapes assumptions about future behaviour. Social capital is a moral resource that increases with use (Putnam, 2000). The growth of generalized trust is a function of everyday compliance with norms, and the more individuals cooperate with each other, the more they trust one another. Past experiences of reliable cooperative interaction tends to enhance our general sense of the trustworthiness of other people. In short, trustworthiness routinely generates trust, and conversely lack of reciprocity tends to deflate trust. In societies where there is relatively low trust, bureaucratic and legal measures will become the dominant mechanisms for securing social order. It has been our contention that Singapore is a low-trust society in which, because the state does not trust independent social groups in society, all forms of criticism or opposition are regarded as anarchic and dangerous.

Managing religions and the enclave society

Many of these liberal approaches assume the development of societies towards multiculturalism in which open borders and significant geographical mobility can be taken for granted. Having discussed the liberal model at some length, we shall conclude with a far more pessimistic vision of modern societies in terms of a theory of social enclaves. The problem of managing religion in modern society therefore becomes a problem of managing enclaves, and thereby to limit the contact between such enclaves. This pessimistic view of social change must start with a critique of the whole notion of modern mobility.

In a context of risk and uncertainty, there is a 'paradigm of suspicion' – a defining characteristic of low-trust societies – in which various categories of persons are seen to be dangerous, and hence their movements need to be contained and curtailed. Hence there is a need to conceptualize globalization as also involving 'closure, entrapment and containment' (Shamir, 2005: 199). The result is an emerging system for the management and containment of risk that has a global reach. If we regard the right to be mobile as a resource, it is clear that the risks of insecurity are unequally shared by the population and hence there is a 'mobility gap' that is somewhat similar to the 'information gap' and the 'digital divide'. Finally, there is a clear development of these systems from basic techniques such as building walls and fences to more complex systems involving the use of forensic medicine and bio-profiling (Agamben, 1998).

We have distinguished between two types of enclavement. The first can be called 'spontaneous enclavement' which includes the cultural practices of social groups resulting in social closure as a consequence of intra-social marriage or 'homogamy'. The second type is what we might call 'institutional enclavement'. This type refers to various forms of involuntary social closure, most often by the state with the aim of exclusion. Institutional enclavement can be benign including gated communities to protect vulnerable groups or quarantine to protect social groups from infectious diseases such as avian flu or it may be malicious. Benign enclosure is often in response to short-term risks, while malevolent enclavement includes the use of concentration camps or physical branding to demoralize or destroy a minority community.

With globalization and the problem of security, rather than increasing mobility, we can detect the emergence of an immobility regime of gated communities for the elderly, ghettoes for migrants, legal and illegal, imprisonment and a range of related practices (branding and tagging) for criminals and deviants, and increasingly the need for quarantine to ensure biological containment against bird flu, TB, SARS and HIV. At an everyday level, there are also many illustrations of such spatial closures. As we have suggested, many of these can be benign: frequent-flyer lounges, prayer rooms and no-smoking areas in airports, or women-only carriages on Japanese railways. Many of these practices are ancient (such as the Great Wall of China and quarantine in plague-stricken medieval Europe), but with modern information technology, microbiological innovations and nanotechnology there are a range of new techniques available to states – in particular to control global flows and networks of slavery, crime, terrorism, contraband and warlordism. The causes of the rise of enclave society are numerous – globalization of crime, 'the return of the state', securitization, illegal migration, political paranoia and technical innovations.

Modern enclavement can assume three principal forms: sequestration, storage and seclusion. The isolation or sequestration of populations is the most basic form of social regulation with the aim of protecting host populations from disease or from dangerous persons. By contrast, gated communities to protect the elderly or the vulnerable are designed, not just to keep potential threats on the outside, but to protect these communities from intimate dangers such as self harm. With the ageing of the populations of the developed world and increasing life expectancy, a range of strategies have emerged for the management of the elderly; these include the growth of overseas retirement villages such as Japanese retirement centres in Thailand, homes for the elderly and increasingly luxury cruise ships for the retired in search of medical cures and recuperation. Because it is unlikely that the more aged will ever effectively return to the labour force, these strategies may be conceptualized as forms of 'social storage'. Finally there are a range of new laws and technologies which allow states to categorize and track individuals who are deemed to be dangerous in order to bring about their spatial seclusion. The unemployable and the undesirable typically fall into a category of persons whose actions can come to be regarded as constituting 'offensive behaviour' (Turner, 2006d). In the United Kingdom, the Anti-Social Behaviour Act has given extraordinary powers to the authorities to create zones from which persons deemed to be likely to cause an offence can be excluded. The Act also introduced penalties for beggars by making begging a notifiable offence. The Act creates provisions, not to solve or eradicate crimes, but to put them outside the gaze of virtuous citizens, thereby achieving an emotional seclusion. In Singapore, the government has in fact attempted to avoid urban enclavement through its housing, residential and other policies with the intention of mixing the races. But its policy of maintaining the demographic balance between the three principal groups results paradoxically in what we might call enclavement through bureaucratic classification.

In the modern world religious identities are often transnational offering alternative frameworks for self identification. These self definitions are not produced
by the state. As a consequence, there may be tensions between the transnational
identities of fundamental religions on the one hand and the political identities of
national citizenship. In the American pattern of assimilation, Protestant, Catholic
and Jew were alternative identities within a common pattern of civil religion. In
Europe, however, there is no civil religion as such to which Muslim Europeans or
Christian Europeans or Hindu Europeans could become culturally or emotionally
attached. The idea of European common citizenship has been, at least for the time
being, delayed by the rejection of the Constitution in the referenda in France and the
Netherlands, and by the failure to agree on a common economic budget. This neg-
ative vote may also result in the termination of the process to bring Turkey into the
European Union. Associated with this no vote there is a deep concern about the
expansion of radical Islam into Europe, and the consequence of any delay in
Turkish membership is to define Fortress Europe as primarily a Christian enclave
(Delanty, 2006).

Since 9/11 diasporic Muslim communities around the world have increasingly
been the target of government interventions, social surveys, political investigations
and popular criticism. The traditional indifference or benign neglect of
governments has been replaced by sudden and intense activity. Because the idea
of 'managing Muslims' would be regarded as discriminatory, these forms of
governmentality are often couched in neutral terminology – pluralism, liberalism
or multiculturalism. In this book we have examined the extreme poles of the
new management of religions from liberal policies of upgrading (such as the allo-
cation of resources for education and legislation for group rights) to more extreme
policies of containment and seclusion which we have called policies of enclavement. A liberal policy of upgrading is benign in comparison to enclavement but it
can also lead ultimately to winning 'the war for Muslim minds' (Kepel, 2004).
Enclavement will inevitably produce greater alienation of Muslim communities
from their host societies, but management through seclusion appears to be the
dominant pattern in association with a war on terrorism. The policy of
upgrading can be successful, where it receives support from religious communities
and their intellectuals who would prefer some level of secular modernization over
more traditional emphases on commitment to customary practices. In comparative
global terms, the resources, status and performance of Muslim societies in
education, especially in higher education, is poor, and hence a reformist strategy
of improving the educational attainment of Muslims is highly desirable
(Hassan, 2006).

Conclusion: the Singapore model

The Singapore government is acutely aware of its own internal and external security issues given the size and location of the island. In one sense there is no longer
any difference between foreign and domestic policies, since security requires managing both successfully. The security issue for Singapore hinges to a large extent on

sustaining 'racial harmony' internally and avoiding security threats emerging in the region around racial and ethnic conflict. Managing religions is in this sense an important plank in its foreign policy orientation. Because as we have argued Singapore is a low-trust society, its approach to social management is very explicit and often heavy handed. Social harmony in Singapore requires a variety of policies that are intended to sustain the status quo, which requires maintaining the demographic balance between the existing ethnic groups. Such a policy is difficult to develop and install, and so far attempts to boost the middle class, and therefore Chinese, fertility rate have been unsuccessful. Singapore's current fertility rate of 1.3 is among the lowest in Asia and of course 'the Malay problem' is also a demographic problem.

Has Singapore been successful in its ethnic and religious policies? The PAP government has during its time of continuous government enjoyed one crucial strategic advantage. If its policies failed in some significant manner during the early years of independence – economic crisis, loss of confidence, a crisis of leadership and civil unrest – Singapore would have been absorbed back into the Malay federation and the Chinese majority would have become the Chinese minority. Racial antagonism between the Chinese and Malay communities has been a more or less permanent feature of modern Malay history at least since the 1940s and was an important factor in the struggle against communism because the British were able to appeal to Malay nationalism against the communist insurgency. The Chinese majority in Singapore have a very strong interest in the ongoing success of PAP policies – economic, political and social. The Islamization of Malaysia has provided the backdrop to Singaporean secularization policies. While the PAP can control the situation at a public level, the destabilization of the religious field by vigorous competition between Christian evangelism and Muslim revivalism may in the long run prove difficult to regulate.

Singapore is of interest to political sociologists because it represents an interesting model of authoritarian, but largely successful, management and as such is taken as the harbinger of the future demise of democracy. This authoritarianism is not unique to Singapore. According to Harvey the 'connection between dictatorial rule and neo-liberal economics has already been well documented' for South Korea, Taiwan and Singapore, but this connection is perhaps most obvious in the Singaporean case (2006: 34). This connection between politics and neo-liberalism has been famously expressed by Danilo Zolo (2001) as the 'Singapore model'. Zolo argues, following Ralf Dahrendorf, that the societies of western Europe were in the post-war period relatively successful because they combined the production of resources to sustain a welfare state, safeguard national identities and protect fundamental rights. Globalization has in many ways undermined these three conditions. As the economy has become global, states no longer exercise effective control over corporations and hence the tax basis of welfare is often eroded. We might add that ageing populations have contributed to this welfare crisis because pensions cannot be adequately sustained. National identities have been challenged by migration creating complex multicultural societies, and finally states have often retreated from the protection of rights in favour of security and bureaucratic surveillance.

Singapore may represent at least one illustration of the evolution of this post-democratic trend because Zolo argues in Singapore 'political representation is more than ever a procedural pretence since the power is irreversibly held by the bureaucratic and administrative apparatus' (2001: 412). Substantial oppositional parties do not really exist and there is no serious public debate on politics, race or religion. Thus, one fundamental aspect of the Singapore model is that the management of religions might prevent genuine dialogue between religious groups. Any dialogue is organized by the state such as MUIS and represents a top-down 'conversation' between spokespeople selected in advance by the state, rather than any real meaningful dialogue between practitioners.

Singapore is sociologically interesting because it represents an almost unique case study providing evidence for the perennial sociological question: how is society possible? Many sociologists, following the sociological theories of Talcott Parsons, are inclined to argue that in the last analysis a society exists because it shares common values. Given Singapore's history of multiculturalism, it is unlikely that Singapore is held together in any significant way by a shared culture. Certainly we could not seriously believe that it has a common religious culture, since as we have seen Singaporean society is deeply fragmented around religious loyalties. On the other hand, we would certainly not want to propose that the island society is held together by coercive measures. It is true that there is an ever present police force and quasi-military force on the streets, MRT and airport, and there is a coercive use of the law courts to control opposition and resistance, but this situation is very far removed from the coercive experiences of eastern European communist societies or contemporary China. As part of our conclusion to this study, we suggest that one important element of Singaporean solidarity is neither cultural nor political, but economic. Perhaps the social glue of Singapore lies ultimately in its pension scheme.

The Central Provident Fund (CPF) is a mechanism whereby every citizen has to contribute towards provision for old age and sickness. This fund can also help individuals to purchase a property or finance an extra educational qualification. The system is crucial to citizenship since it encourages individuals to be responsible for their futures. Both employees and employers are compelled to make contributions to the scheme and, while the CPF has its own board, it is definitely subordinate to government plans. The policy has greatly facilitated home ownership and almost 90 per cent of policy holders have raised mortgages through the scheme. One important aspect of CPF provisions is the availability of free medical care in retirement. Elsewhere in the modern world where there is a considerable fear of the so-called 'ratio of dependency' namely the number of retired persons in relation to those of employable age, the implicit social contract in pension-welfare arrangements has been challenged by the prospect of privatization. In contrast, the CPF is an economic and social contract that locks the worker into the society by securing their future well-being in return for their contributions. If pensions are collective arrangements that underpin social solidarity, then the CPF is a powerful mechanism for ensuring that individuals, regardless of race or religion, have a shared investment in the continuity of Singapore as a society. Through these means, the

Singaporean state 'promotes social inclusion hand in hand with social control' (Blackburn, 2002: 263).

While promoting social inclusion through economic success, the Singaporean state also relies on key measures of authoritarian regulation. What then is to be done by liberal states to foster tolerance and civil harmony? Positive state policies towards minorities cannot succeed unless there are parallel social changes in civil society that create new patterns of social solidarity that are strong enough to cross enclaves. First, a successful society that is diverse and complex needs a strong legal framework and effective citizenship to create a public environment in which overt and blatant racism is not tolerated and where assumptions about cultural diversity are core elements of government business. Governments need such explicit policies that convey to the public the principle that the government does not favour one ethnic or religious group over another, and hence minority rights are clearly protected by the law. Second there must be sufficient economic growth and an adequate welfare and taxation system to redistribute resources in such a way that second-generation children of migrant families are not systematically disadvantaged. Educational policies and resources are therefore fundamental to success. Third, there must be a social climate that allows for social reciprocity and the emergence of intermediate associations (clubs, churches and voluntary associations) to build up social capital as the foundation of liberal values. These overlapping social groups are the social support that make possible an overlapping consensus of value and belief. Finally, there must be cultural sphere (including sport and other leisure activities) where general values (Rawls's overlapping consensus) can counteract the tendency towards group loyalty, localism, tribalism or ethnic solidarity. Without these overlapping social groups, any liberal hope of fostering an overlapping consensus is doomed to failure, and enclavement will ensue.

Bibliography

Abdul Aziz Johari (1962) 'The Javanese People of Singapore', Unpublished Academic Exercise: University of Singapore.

Abdullah bin Malim Baginda (1959) 'The Boyanese of Singapore: A study of one of the Indonesian minority groups in Singapore, in order to investigate how far their beliefs, mores and customs serve to maintain the separateness of the group, and to what extent this separateness is increasing or diminishing', Unpublished Academic Exercise: University of Malaya.

Abdullah Yusuf Ali (1989) *The Holy Qur'an: Text, Translation, and Commentary* (4th edn), Brentwood, Md., USA: Amana Corp.

Agamben, G. (1998) *Homo Sacer. Sovereign Power and Bare Life*, Stanford: Stanford University Press.

Alexander, J. C. (2006) *The Civil Sphere*, Oxford: Oxford University Press.

Aljunied, S. M. K. (2009) *Colonialism, Violence and Muslims in Southeast Asia: The Maria Hertogh Controversy and its Aftermath*, London: Routledge.

Allan, G. (1989) *Friendship: Developing a Sociological Perspective*, Hemel Hempstead: Harvester Wheatsheaf.

Al-Qaradawi, Y. (1994) *The Lawful and the Prohibited in Islam* translated by Kamal El-Helbawy, M. Moinuddin Siddiqui, Syed Shukry. Kuwait International Islamic Federation of Student Organizations.

Andaya, B. W. and Andaya, L. Y. (2001) *History of Malaysia* (2nd edn.) Honolulu: University of Hawai'i Press.

Anderson, B. (1983) *Imagined Communities: Reflections on the Origin and Spread of Nationalism*, New York: Verso.

Anderson, B. (2002) *The Spectre of Comparisons: Nationalism, Southeast Asia and the World*, London: Verso.

Appiah, K. A. (2006) *Cosmopolitanism: Ethics in a World of Strangers*, New York: W. W. Norton.

Arendt, H. (1976) *The Origins of Totalitarianism*, San Diego: Harvest Books

Atasoy, Y. (2006) 'Governing Women's Morality: A study of Islamic veiling in Canada', *European Journal of Cultural Studies*, 9 (2): 203–21.

Barr, M. D. (1999) 'Lee Kuan Yew: Races, culture & genes', *Journal of Contemporary Asia*, 29 (2): 145–66.

Barr, M. D. (2000) 'Lee Kuan Yew and the "Asian Values" debate', *Asian Studies Review*, 24 (3): 9–34.

Barry, B. M. (2001) *Culture and Equality: An Egalitarian Critique of Multiculturalism*, Cambridge, MA: Harvard University Press.

Benjamin, G. (1976) 'The Cultural Logic of Singapore's Multiracialism', in Hassan, R. (ed.) *Singapore in Transition*, Singapore: Oxford University Press, 115–33.

Bilveer Singh (2007) *The Talibanization of Southeast Asia: Losing the War on Terror to Islamist Extremists*, Westport, Connecticut: Praeger Security International.

Blackburn, R. (2002) *Banking on Death or Investing in Life*, London: Verso.

Boltanski, L. and Thevenot, L. (2006) *On Justification: Economies of Worth*, Princeton: Princeton University Press.

Bourdieu, P. (1977) *Outline of a Theory of Practice*, Cambridge: Cambridge University Press.

Bourdieu, P. (1984) *Distinction. A Critique of the Judgement of Taste*, London: Routledge and Kegan Paul.

Bourdieu, P. and Wacquant, L. (1992) *An Invitation to Reflexive Sociology*, Cambridge: Polity.

Bowen, J. R. (2007) *Why the French Don't Like Headscarves: Islam, the State, and Public Space*, Princeton: Princeton University Press.

Brenner, S. (1996) 'Reconstructing Self and Society: Javanese Muslim women and the veil', *American Ethnologist*, 23 (4): 693–7.

Brown, D. B. (1994) *The State and Ethnic Politics in Southeast Asia*, London: Routledge.

Butler, J. (2006) *Precarious Life. The Powers of Mourning and Violence*, London: Verso.

Case, W. (2002) *Politics in Southeast Asia: Democracy or Less*, London: RoutledgeCurzon.

Chang, T. C. (1999) 'Local Uniqueness in the Global Village: Heritage tourism in Singapore', *The Professional Geographer*, 51 (1): 91–103.

Charrad, M. M. (1998) 'Cultural Diversity within Islam: Veils and laws in Tunisia', in Bodman, H. L. and Tohidi, N. (eds) *Women in Muslim Societies: Diversity Within Unity*, Boulder and London: Lynne Reinner Publishers.

Chee, M. F. (2006) 'The Historical Evolution of *Madrasah* Education in Singapore', in Noor Aisha, A. R. and Lai, A. E. (eds) *Secularism and Spirituality: Seeking Integrated Knowledge and Success in Madrasah Education in Singapore*, Singapore: Marshall Cavendish Academic, 6–28.

Cheung, P. P. L. (1991) 'Social and Economic Implications of Singapore's Immigration and Emigration Patterns', paper presented at the International Conference on Migration, Centre for Advanced Studies, National University of Singapore.

Chua, B. H. (1995) *Communitarian Ideology and Democracy in Singapore*, London: Routledge.

Chua, B. H. (1997) *Political Legitimacy and Housing: Stakeholding in Singapore*, London: Routledge.

Chua, B. H. (2003) 'Multiculturalism in Singapore: An instrument of social control', *Race & Class*, 44: 58–77.

Chua, B. H. (2004) 'Communitarianism without Competitive Politics in Singapore', in Chua, B. H. (ed.) *Communitarian Politics in Asia*, London: Routledge, 78–101.

Chua, B. H. (2005) 'The Cost of Membership in Ascribed Community', in Kymlicka, W. and He, B. (eds) *Multiculturalism in Asia*, Oxford: Oxford University Press, 170–95.

Chua B. H. and Rajah, A. (2003) 'Food, Ethnicity and Nation', in Chua, B. H. *Life is Not Complete Without Shopping*, Singapore: Singapore University Press, 93–117.

Clammer, J. (1998) *Race and State in Independent Singapore, 1965–1990: The Cultural Politics of Pluralism in a Multiethnic Society*, Aldershot: Ashgate.

Cohen, J. and Arato, A. (1992) *Civil Society and Political Theory*, Cambridge, MIT Press.

Corrigan, P. and Sayer, D. (1985) *The Great Arch. English State Formation as Cultural Revolution*, Oxford: Blackwell.

Dayang Istiasyah Hussein (2003) 'School Effectiveness & Nation-Building in Singapore', Unpublished Masters Thesis, National University of Singapore.

DeBernardi, J. (2008) 'Commodifying Blessings: Celebrating the double yang festival in Penang, Malaysia and Wudang mountain China', in Kitiarsa, P. (ed.) *Religious Commodifications in Asia: Marketing Gods*, London: Routledge, 49–67.

Delanty, G. (2006) 'Borders in a Changing Europe: Dynamics of Openness and Closure', *Comparative European Politics*, 4: 183–202.

De Souza, D. (1980) 'The Politics of Language: Language planning in Singapore', in Afrendas, E. and Kuo, E. (eds) *Language and Society in Singapore*, Singapore: Singapore University Press, 203–32.

Djamour, J. (1965) *Malay Kinship and Marriage in Singapore*, London: The Athlone Press.

Durkheim, È. (2001) *The Elementary Forms of the Religious Life*, Oxford: Oxford University Press.

Fischer, M. M. (1978) 'On Changing the Concept and Position of Persian Women', in Beck, L. and Keddie, N. (eds) *Women in the Muslim World*, Cambridge, MA: Harvard University Press.

Foucault, M. (1977) 'Nietzsche, Genealogy and History', in Bouchard, D. (ed.) *Language, Counter-Memory, Practice*, Ithaca, NY: Cornell University Press, 139–64.

Foucault, M. (2000) 'Governmentality', in *Power: The Essential Works of Michel Foucault, Vol. 3*, London: Allen Lane, 201–22.

Fowler, B. (1997) *Pierre Bourdieu and Cultural Theory: Critical Investigations*, Thousand Oaks: Sage.

Fowler, B. (ed.) (2000) *Reading Bourdieu on Society and Culture*, Oxford: Blackwell.

Fox, J. J. (2004) 'Currents in Contemporary Islam in Indonesia', paper presented at Harvard Asia Vision 21, Harvard University, 29 April–1 May 2004, Cambridge, MA (http://rspas.anu.edu.au/papers/anthropology/04_fox_islam_indonesia.pdf).

Funston, J. (2006) 'Singapore', in Fealy, G. and Hooker, V. (eds) *Voices of Islam in Southeast Asia: A Contemporary Sourcebook*, Singapore: Institute of Southeast Asian Studies.

Furnivall, J. S. (1956) *Colonial Policy and Practice: A Comparative Study of Burma and Netherlands India*, New York: New York University Press.

Ganesan, N. (2004) 'The Political History of Ethnic Relations in Singapore', in Lai, A. E. (ed.) *Beyond Rituals and Riots: Ethnic Pluralism and Social Cohesion in Singapore*, Singapore: Eastern Universities Press.

Glazer, N. (1997) *We Are All Multiculturalists Now*, Cambridge, MA: Harvard University Press.

Goffman, E. (1959) *The Presentation of Self in Everyday Life*, Garden City, New York: Doubleday Anchor.

Goffman, E. (1963) *Behavior in Public Places*, New York: Free Press.

Goffman, E. (1969) *Strategic Interaction*, Oxford: Basil Blackwell.

Goh, D. P. S. (1999) 'Rethinking Resurgent Christianity in Singapore', *Southeast Asian Journal of Social Science*, 27 (1): 89–112.

Gopinathan, S. (1996) 'Globalisation, the State and Education Policy in Singapore', *Asia Pacific Journal of Education*, 16 (1): 74–87.

Gunaratna, R. (2006) 'Introductory Remarks', in *Transnational Islamist Movements in Asia: Networks, Structure and Threat Assessment*, Report of an International Conference jointly organized by the International Centre for Political Violence and Terrorism Research (ICPVTR) at the Institute of Defence and Strategic Studies, Singapore, and Center for Eurasian Policy, the Hudson Institute (US), 19–20 September 2006, Sentosa, Singapore. (http://www.pvtr.org/pdf/Report/ trans%20Islamist%20Movemt.pdf).

Hartmann, D. and Gerteis, J. (2005) 'Dealing with Diversity: Mapping multiculturalism in sociological terms', *Sociological Theory*, 23 (2): 218–40.

Harvey, D. (2006) *Spaces of Global Development*, London: Verso.

Hassan, R. (1971) 'Interethnic Marriage in Singapore: A sociological analysis', *Sociology and Social Research*, 55: 305–23.

Hassan, R. (2006) 'Nations Locked in Servitude by a Gulf in Learning', *The Times Higher Education Supplement*, 2 November.

Hassan, R. and Benjamin, G. (1973) 'Ethnic Outmarriage Rates in Singapore: The influence of traditional socio-cultural organization', *Journal of Marriage and the Family*, 35 (4): 731–8.

Heaton, T. B. and Pratt, E. L. (1990) 'The Effects of Religious Homogamy on Marital Satisfaction and Stability', *Journal of Family Issues*, 11 (2): 191–207.

Hefner, R. (2000) *Civil Islam: Muslims and Democratization in Indonesia*, Princeton: Princeton University Press.

Heng, J. (2002) 'Understanding Words and Knowing Men', in Chan, A. K. L. (ed.) *Mencius. Contexts and Interpretations*, Honolulu: University of Hawai'i Press, 151–68.

Hill, M. (2002) *The Elite-Sponsored Moral Panic: A Singapore Perspective*, Singapore: Centre for Advanced Studies, 21–4.

Hill, M. and Lian, K. F. (1995) *The Politics of Nation Building and Citizenship in Singapore*, London: Routledge.

Hodgson, M. G. S. (1974) *The Venture of Islam. Conscience and History in a World Civilization, Volume 2, The Expansion of Islam in the Middle Periods*, Chicago and London: University of Chicago Press.

Hui, W. T. (1992) 'Singapore's Immigration Policy: An economic perspective', in Low, L. and Toh, M. H. (eds) *Public Policies in Singapore, Changes in the 1980s and Future Signposts*, Singapore: Times Academic Press, 170–93.

Huntington, S. P. (1993) 'The Clash of Civilizations', *Foreign Affairs*, 72 (3): 22–48.

Huntington, S. P. (1996) *The Clash of Civilizations and the Remaking of World Order*, New York: Simon & Schuster.

Hussin Mutalib (2005) 'Singapore Muslims: The quest for identity in a modern city state', *Journal of Muslim Minority Affairs*, 25 (1): 53–72.

Joppke, C. (2004) 'The Retreat of Multiculturalism in the Liberal State: Theory and policy', *British Journal of Sociology*, 55 (2): 237–57.

Kamaludeen Bin Mohamed Nasir (2007a) 'Rethinking the "Malay Problem" in Singapore: Image, rhetoric and social realities', *Journal of Muslim Minority Affairs*, 27 (2): 309–18.

Kamaludeen Bin Mohamed Nasir (2007b) 'The Muslim Power Elites in Singapore: The burden of a community', Masters Thesis, Department of Sociology, National University of Singapore.

Kamaludeen Bin Mohamed Nasir and Aljunied, S. M. K. (2009) *Muslims as Minorities: History and Social Realities of Muslims in Singapore*, Kuala Lumpur: National University of Malaysia Press.

Kepel, G. (2002) *Jihad. The Trail of Political Islam*, London: I. B. Tauris.

Kepel, G. (2004) *The War for Muslim Minds. Islam and the West*, Cambridge, MA: The Belknap Press.

Kymlicka, W. (1995) *Multicultural Citizenship: A Liberal Theory of Minority Rights*, Oxford: Oxford University Press.

Lai, A. E. (1995) *Meanings of Multiethnicity: A Case Study of Ethnicity and Ethnic Relations*, Kuala Lumpur: Oxford University Press.

Lau, D. C. (ed.) (2004) *Mencius*, London: Penguin.

Lazerwitz, B. (1981) 'Jewish-Christian marriages and conversions', *Jewish Social Studies*, (43): 31–46.

Lee, K. Y. (2001) *From Third World to First: The Singapore Story, 1965–2000*, New York: HarperCollins Publishers.

Lee, S. M. (1988) 'Intermarriage and Ethnic Relations in Singapore', *Journal of Marriage and the Family*, 50 (1): 255–65.

Leila Hessini (1994) 'Wearing the Hijab in Contemporary Morocco: Choice and identity' in Fatma, M. G. and Shiva, B. (eds) *Reconstructing Gender in the Middle East: Tradition, Identity, and Power*, New York: Columbia University Press.

Levy, J. (2000) *The Multiculturalism of Fear*, Oxford: Oxford University.

Li, T. (1989) *Malays in Singapore: Culture, Economy, and Ideology*, Singapore: Oxford University Press.

Lian, K. F. (1999) 'Migration and the Formation of Malaysia and Singapore', in Cohen, R. (ed.) *The Cambridge Survey Of World Migration*, 392–6.

Lily Zubaidah Rahim (1998) *The Singapore Dilemma: The Political and Educational Marginality of the Malay Community*, Kuala Lumpur: Oxford University Press.

Locke, J. (1946) *The Second Treatise of Government* (edited with an introduction by J. W. Gough), Oxford: B. Blackwell.

Mahathir bin Mohamad (1982) *The Malay Dilemma*, Kuala Lumpur: Federal Publications.

Mahmood, S. (2005) *Politics of Piety. The Islamic Revival and the Feminist Subject*, Princeton and Oxford: Princeton University Press.

Mariam Mohamed Ali (1990) *Uniformity and Diversity among Muslims in Singapore*, Masters Thesis, Dept of Sociology, National University of Singapore.

Martinez, P. (2001) 'Malaysia in 2000: A year of contradictions', *Asian Survey*, 41 (1): 189–200.

Mauzy, D. K. and Milne, R. S. (1986) *Malaysia: Tradition, Modernity, and Islam*, Boulder: Westview.

Mauzy, D. K. and Milne, R. S. (2002) *Singapore Politics under the People's Action Party*, London: Routledge.

Mendaki (2007) *Progress of the Malay Community since 1980*, Singapore: Mendaki.

Mohamad Abu Bakar (1981) 'Islamic Revivalism and the Political Process in Malaysia', *Asian Survey*, 21 (10): 1040–59.

Mukhlis Abu Bakar (2006) 'Between State Interests and Citizen Rights: Whither the Madrasah?', in Noor Aisha, A. R. and Lai, A. E. (eds) *Secularism and Spirituality: Seeking Integrated Knowledge and Success in Madrasah Education in Singapore*, Singapore: Marshall Cavendish Academic, 29–57.

Nagata, J. A. (1984) *The Reflowering of Malaysian Islam: Modern Religious Radicals and their Roots*, Vancouver: University of British Columbia Press.

Nakanishi, H. (1998) 'Power, Ideology, and Women's Consciousness in Postrevolutionary Iran', in Bodman, H. and Tohibi, N. (eds) *Women in Muslim Societies*, Boulder and London: Lynne Reinner Publishers, 83–100.

Noor Aisha Abdul Rahman (2006) 'The Aims of Madrasah Education in Singapore: Problems and perceptions', in Noor Aisha, A. R. and Lai, A. E. (eds) *Secularism and Spirituality: Seeking Integrated Knowledge and Success in Madrasah Education in Singapore*, Singapore: Marshall Cavendish Academic, 58–92.

Parsons, T. (1999) 'Belief, Unbelief and Disbelief', in Turner, B. S. (ed.) *The Talcott Parsons Reader*, Oxford: Blackwell, 51–79.

Pereira, A. A. (2000) 'State Collaboration with Transnational Corporations: The Case of Singapore's industrial programmes (1965–1999)', *Competition and Change*, 4 (4): 423–51.

Pereira, A. A. (2005) 'Religiosity and Economic Development in Singapore', *Journal of Contemporary Religion*, 20 (2): 161–78.

Pereira, A. A. (2008) 'Manufacturing Human Resources: The role of the social investment state', in Lian, K. F. and Tong, C. K. (eds) *Social Policy in Post-Industrial Singapore*, Leiden: Brill, 121–44.

PERGAS (2004) *Moderation in Islam: In the Context of Muslim Community in Singapore*, Singapore: PERGAS.

Purushotam, N. (1998) 'Disciplining Difference: "Race" in Singapore', in Kahn, J. S. (ed.) *Southeast Asian Identities: Culture and the Politics of Representation in Indonesia, Malaysia, Singapore and Thailand*, Singapore: ISEAS, 51–94.

Putnam, R. D. (2000) *Bowling Alone. The Collapse and Revival of American Community*, New York: Simon & Schuster.

Rawls, J. (1971) *Theory of Justice*, Cambridge, MA: The Belknap Press.

Rawls, J. (2001) *The Law of Peoples*, Cambridge, MA: Harvard University Press.

Riaz, M. N. and Chaudry, M. M. (2004) *Halal Food Production*, Boca Raton, Fla.: CRC Press.

Rinakit, S. and Soesastro, H. (1998) 'Indonesia', in Morrison, C. E. and Soesastro, H. (eds) *Domestic Adjustments to Globalization*, Tokyo and New York: Japan Center for International Exchange, 193–206.

Rojek, C. and Turner, B. S. (2000) 'Decorative Sociology: A critique of the cultural turn', *The Sociological Review*, 48: 629–48.

Roy, O. (2004) *Globalised Islam: The Search for a New Ummah*, London: Hurst and Co.

Rumsford, C. (2006) 'Theorizing Borders', *European Journal of Social Theory*, 9 (2): 155–69.

Sadri, M. and Sadri, A. (eds) (2000) *Reason, Freedom and Democracy in Islam: The Essential Writings of Abdolkarim Soroush*, Oxford: Oxford University Press.

Sassen, S. (1999) *Guests and Aliens*, New York: The New Press.

Satha-Anand, C. (2005) *The Life of this World: Negotiated Muslims Lives in Thai Society*, Singapore: Marshall Cavendish Academic.

Schmitt, C. (1996) *The Concept of the Political*, Chicago and London: University of Chicago Press.

Shamir, Ronen (2005) 'Without Borders? Notes on globalization as a mobility regime', *Sociological Theory*, 23 (2): 197–217.

Shamsul, A. B. (2001) 'A History of an Identity an Identity of a History: The idea and practice of "Malayness" in Malaysia reconsidered', *Journal of Southeast Asian Studies*, 32 (3): 355–66.

Shamsul, A. B. (2005) 'Islam Embedded: Religion and plurality in Southeast Asia as a mirror for Europe', *Asia Europe Journal*, 3 (2): 159–78.

Shilling, C. (1993) *The Body and Social Theory*, Thousand Oaks: Sage.

Simmel, G. (1950) *The Sociology of Georg Simmel*, translated and edited by Kurt H. Wolff, Glencoe, Ill. Free Press.

Singapore Department of Statistics (2001) *Census of Population 2000: Demographic Characteristics*, Singapore: Dept. of Statistics.

Singapore Department of Statistics (2007) *Yearbook of Statistics 2006*, Singapore: Dept. of Statistics.

Singapore Ministry of Education (2006) *Education Statistics Digest 2005*, Singapore: Ministry of Education (http://www.moe.gov.sg/esd/ESD2006.pdf).

Singapore Ministry of Home Affairs (2003) *The Jemaah Islamiyah Arrests and the Threat of Terrorism*, White Paper, Singapore: MHA (http://www.mha.gov.sg/get_blob.aspx?file_id=252_complete.pdf).

Sinha, V. (1999) 'Constituting and Reconstituting the Religious Domain in the Modern Nation-State of Singapore', in Kwok, K-W., Kwa, C. G., Kong, L. and Yeoh, B. (eds) *Our Place in Time: Exploring Heritage and Memory in Singapore*, Singapore: Singapore Heritage Society, 76–95.

Smith, W. C. (1957) *Islam in Modern History*, Princeton: Princeton University Press.

Stimpfl, J. (2006) 'Growing up Malay in Singapore', in Lian, K. F. (ed.) *Race, Ethnicity, and the State in Malaysia and Singapore*, Leiden: Brill, 61–94.

Sullivan, G. and Gunasekaran, S. (1994) 'Motivations of Migrants from Singapore to Australia', *Field Report Series* No 28, Institute of Southeast Asian Studies.

Sutton, P. W. and Vertigans, S. (2005) *Resurgent Islam: A Sociological Approach*, Cambridge: Polity.

Suzaina Kadir (2004) 'Islam, State and Society in Singapore', *Inter-Asia Cultural Studies*, 5 (3): 357–71.

Suzaina Kadir (2005) 'The Role of Education in Ethnic/Religious Conflict Management: The Singapore case', *ICIP Journal*, 2 (1): 1–18.

Tan, E. S. (2004) *Does Class Matter? Social Stratification and Orientations in Singapore*, Singapore: World Scientific.

Taylor, P. (2007) *Cham Muslims of the Mekong Delta: Place and Mobility in the Cosmopolitan Periphery*, Singapore: NUS Press.

Taylor, P. (ed.) (2007) *Modernity and Re-enchantment. Religion in Post-revolutionary Vietnam*, Singapore: ISEAS.

Tong, J. K. C. (2008) 'McDonaldization and the Megachurches: A case study of City Harvest Church Singapore', in Kitiarsa, P. (ed.) *Religious Commodifications in Asia: Marketing Gods*, London: Routledge, 186–204.

Tong, J. K. C. and Turner, B. S. (2008) 'Women, Piety and Practice: A study of women and religious practice in Malaysia', *Contemporary Islam*, 2 (1): 41–59.

Torpey, J. (1999) *The Invention of the Passport: Surveillance Citizenship and the State*, Cambridge: Cambridge University Press.

Turnbull, C. M. (1989) *A History of Singapore: 1819–1988*, Kuala Lumpur: Oxford University Press.

Turner, B. S. (1991) *Religion and Social Theory* (2nd edn), London: Sage.

Turner, B. S. (1992) *Regulating Bodies: Essays in Medical Sociology*, London: Routledge.

Turner, B. S. (2000) 'An Outline of a General Sociology of the Body', in Turner, B.S. (ed.) *The Blackwell Companion to Social Theory* (2nd edn), Malden, MA: Blackwell, 480–501.

Turner, B. S. (2006a) 'Citizenship and the Crisis of Multiculturalism', *Citizenship Studies*, 10 (5): 607–18.

Turner, B. S. (2006b) *Vulnerability and Rights*, PA: Penn State University Press.

Turner, B. S. (2006c) 'Religion', *Theory, Culture & Society*, 23 (2–3): 437–55.

Turner, B. S. (2006d) 'Social Capital, Trust and Offensive Behaviour', in von Hirsch, A. and Semester, A. P. (eds) *Incivilities: Regulating Offensive Behaviour*, Oxford and Portland: Hart Publishing, 219–38.

Turner, B. S. (2007a) 'Religious Diversity and the Liberal Consensus', in Turner, B. S. (ed.) *Religious Diversity in Civil Society*, Oxford: Bardwell Press, 49–71.

Turner, B. S. (2007b) 'Managing Religions: State responses to religious diversity', *Contemporary Islam*, 1 (2): 123–37.

Turner, B. S. (2008) 'Introduction: The price of piety', *Contemporary Islam*, 2 (1): 1–6.

Vasil, R. K (2000) *Governing Singapore: Democracy and National Development*, Singapore: Allen & Unwin.

Vasil, R. K. (2004) *A Citizen's Guide to Government and Politics in Singapore*, Singapore: Tatisman Pub.

Wan Hussin Zoohri (1990) *The Singapore Malays: The Dilemma of Development*, Singapore: Kesatuan Guru-Guru Melayu Singapura.

Weber, M. (1952) *Ancient Judaism*, New York: Free Press.

World Values Survey (Singapore) (2002) (http://www.worldvaluessurvey.org/).

Yap, M. T. (1991) 'Singaporeans Overseas: A study of emigrants in Australia and Canada', *IPS Reports Series, Report No. 3*, The Institute of Policy Studies.

Yeoh, B. (1996) *Contesting Space: Singapore: Power Relations and the Urban Built Environment in Colonial Singapore*, Kuala Lumpur: Oxford University Press.

Zolo, D. (2001) 'The Singapore Model: Democracy, communication and globalization', in Nash, K. and Scott, A. (eds) *The Blackwell Companion to Political Sociology*, Oxford: Blackwell, 407–17.

Zuraidah Ibrahim (1994) *Muslims in Singapore: A Shared Vision*, Singapore: Majlis Ugama Islam Singapura (MUIS).

Index